Call Me Worthy

Unlocking a Painful Past
For a Glorious Future

Dr. Anne Worth

Call Me Worthy
By Dr. Anne Worth

Back cover photo by Helen Meyer.
Cover design by Frank Ball

Seventh Printing

Published by:
Dr. Anne Worth
CallMeWorthy@gmail.com

TO MY ADOPTED CHILDREN

GOD'S MOST PRECIOUS GIFT

Contents

The Glory Years

Appreciations

The simple words, "thank you," seem dreadfully inadequate to express my gratitude to those who helped me survive until I met the one who would save me. With heartfelt appreciation, I thank:

- My Aunts, who loved me unconditionally and always (Annie, Jewell, Tooie, Virginia, Hazel, Sue, Irene and Sis).

- My cousins, especially Barbara and Gale, the sisters I never had.

- Anna Sewell, author of *Black Beauty*, who gave me a deep empathy for the plight of animals.

- Dottie Doyle, my safe haven.

- My adopted children:
  — Linda, who blessed me with the privilege of being her mother, grandmother to Katherine and Anna, and great-grandmother to Layla and Francesca.
  — Dusty, my daughter, waiting in Heaven.
  — Anton, my loving Russian son and the sweetest man I know.

— Michael, my Sudanese son who found this world too painful, but true to his heritage is tending God's cattle on a thousand hills.

- Pat Love, my fun-loving cheerleader.

- Pia Mellody, the therapist who taught me about shame and worth.

- Starla Bruce, who carried me through some of my most challenging years.

- Martha Hook, one of my first and dearest Christian friends.

- Ryanne Leigh and Jeff Darland, the couple who invited me to attend the Barnabas Journey workshop.

- Bill Counts, the man in the other chair and my spiritual father.

- Connie Freeman, who knew just what to do during the Barnabas Journey workshop.

- Joyce Meyer, television evangelist, who humorously taught me to live and love the Christian life.

- The Followers and the Go-Girls, those sassy, praying sisters who welcomed me into the fold.

- Precious Cindy Forester, the one nearest to my heart.

- Charlynn Johns, BFF, who knows my heart.

- Joe and Sarah, who have graciously and generously opened their home to me over many years.

- My parents, who gave me life and passed down the qualities of grit, determination, and creativity. I wish they had found peace.

I have immense gratitude to those who helped bring *Call Me Worthy* to life.

- Teresa Velardi, the first person who encouraged me to write *Call Me Worthy*. She understood my message and encouraged me spiritually and lovingly every step of the way.

- Roaring Lambs Ministry, for including my Scripture testimony in *Stories of Roaring Faith, Volume 4*.

- Beverly Parkhurst Moss, comrade in arms, who helped with the early writing of *Call Me Worthy*.

- Tracy Barry, who provided excellent last-minute editing and support.

- Frank Ball, who was the most significant help in getting this book to press.

Although many of the relationships described in this book were hurtful, there are no "bad people" in my story. Hurting people hurt people. Everyone, including the author, is loved and forgiven.

Foreword

We can learn a great deal from reading Dr. Anne Worth's story. She describes how growing up in a dysfunctional family environment resulted in bitterness toward God and years of poor life choices.

I was present the day Anne turned her life over to Jesus as her Savior. I remember looking into her angry, doubting eyes before she trusted Jesus. Her bitterness had alienated her from God for fifty-five years. Without God to guide her, she made one desperate, defeating decision after another.

Many times in her past she thought she had found the path to happiness, and I feared her decision might last only a few months. Without a quick miracle, she might move on to something else. But she grew in her faith and has never wavered in her dependence and trust in Jesus.

The Bible has many examples of Jesus reaching out to women who were outcasts. Despite their sinful ways, Jesus saw them as lost girls in need of a father. They were treated as the lowest of the low by society, but the love of Jesus elevated them to their true created identity as daughters of the King of the Universe. As a result, they helped others believe in the goodness of God. Anne was like one of those women. Jesus touched her heart and changed her, just like he has been touching the hearts of suffering women for 2,000 years.

An important aspect of Anne's book speaks to how the church can be its own worst enemy. Modern day Christians may view themselves in the same arrogant way as the Pharisees of old; only they are devout, righteous, and holy. From their pious position, they condemn others. Such people hurt Anne deeply and sent her fleeing from the church. She ran to places the "angels fear to tread," but God pursued her—even into the ashram of an Indian guru. God stormed the gates of her resistance and misguided searching.

Anne's story is a message of hope. Instead of remaining as she was, hopeless and defeated, she chose to follow Jesus, and he gave her a new life, a new mind, and a new heart. She realized that God had created her for a purpose, and as she pursued that purpose, her life had meaning.

God gives us the gifts and talents necessary to fulfill his assignment. He asked Anne to write his story to tell others that he is the true Father to every person he created. God is waiting to embrace them and give them new life. I believe you will be blessed by reading her victorious life story.

— William Counts; AB, ThM, MA, D.Min, Senior Pastor Emeritus, Fellowship Bible Church, Dallas, Texas

Preface

No matter what you have done,
No matter what has been done to you,
No matter how life locked you up
Or knocked you down,
No matter what,
You can be set free.
To the extreme I was thrown down,
I am lifted up;
To the extreme I was rejected,
I am embraced;
To the extreme I was lost,
I am found.
My heart was set free by God,
Who gives us
Everything the world cannot give.
I thank Him every day.
This is my story.

The Early Years

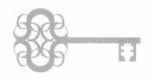

Mother

On the day you were born, you were unwanted.
Ezekiel 16:5

At 7:55 a.m. on a lazy Sunday morning in Oahu, Hawaii, imperial Japanese forces attacked the United States naval base in Pearl Harbor. The majority of the population was probably looking forward to a day of rest when, without warning, the quiet was shattered by the sound of bombs exploding from multiple sites. In a little over one hour, 3,400 Americans lay wounded or dead, many at the bottom of the Pacific Ocean.

The next day in their small-town apartment, my parents sat glued to the radio to hear Franklin Delano Roosevelt declare December 7, 1941, as the "date that will live in infamy." The president petitioned Congress for a declaration of war, and his request passed quickly. Headlines around the world read: U.S. DECLARES WAR!

Millions of patriotic

civilians rushed to volunteer or got drafted into the Armed Forces. From movie stars to schoolboys, men and women in every state, every economic and social stratum, and every age wanted in on the fight.

My father was no exception. Because his stateside job provided transportation vital to the war effort, he could have stayed out of combat. But like most Americans, he was itching to fight for the Red, White, and Blue.

Signing up almost certainly meant he would be in harm's way. The danger of him going into combat panicked her. Loving her, he rescued her from a lifetime of emotional insecurity. Growing up in a tense, cold childhood home caused her to feel adrift and alone. He was her life raft, her life raft. She begged him not to go. The possibility of his death shattered her sense of safety. She begged him not to go. "If you are killed, what will happen to me? Don't you know how I need you? Why would you leave me when you don't have to go? Don't you love me?"

Her fears were real. By the end of World War II, some 242,000 brave Americans would be killed on foreign soil, and untold numbers would suffer physical and mental wounds that would last a lifetime.

An idea began to percolate in her mind: he wanted children. If she got pregnant, the military might exempt him from the draft. Even if he was drafted, having a child might keep him from being sent overseas. Although she doubted her ability to be a caring mother, the possibility of making him happy and keeping him with her made it worth the risk. She had secretly used birth control for their entire marriage, but now she hoped to conceive. Three months after war was declared, I was conceived. I don't think it was a coincidence.

He'll be so proud, she thought, *maybe I can give him a son. Surely he wouldn't leave his namesake to go off for some war in another country.*

Everyone in the family, especially my father, was happy and excited when she announced a little bundle of joy was on the way. Almost simultaneously, the Battle of Midway changed everything. The naval victory created a new level of enthusiasm that the war would be won because of America. Nothing would keep my father from being part of the winning team.

Although he was thrilled to be a father and worried about leaving his wife with a new baby, he knew she would have help from her family. He waited until my birth, but his plans were made. He proudly enlisted in the United States Army.

My mother never forgave him. On the day of his funeral fifty-three years later, she would tell the story of his abandonment one last time.

Almost on the spot, the Army sent him to boot camp and then to extended jungle training. After a short leave when I was five months old, he was deployed to the South Pacific. My mother reluctantly moved back into her parents' house. It would be almost three years before we saw him again. Those years were a tough time for her.

Her insecurity and misery began with the disaffection in her parents' unhappy marriage. Her mother was cold and stiff and seemed to hate her father. She alternately uttered curses at him under her breath or acted as if he didn't exist. My grandmother may have invented the term "ghosting." The home environment was caustic and tense.

3

Something was very wrong, but it was never discussed in the open.

As far back as elementary school, mother was able to escape some of the stress in her home by visiting her affectionate aunt and uncle, who lived right across the street from her parents. Walking home from school every afternoon, she detoured past her house and ran straight into the open arms of her aunt.

After enjoying homemade cookies and milk, her attentive aunt sat by her in the sunny breakfast nook while completing her homework. When they were through, Rosie, the rotund cook with the big smile, served hot iron-skillet cornbread, fresh turnip greens, sliced beefsteak tomatoes, and black-eyed peas from the garden. She was filled up in every way and quietly slipped back into the house where she lived after supper.

Every Friday morning, she got up early and packed her small suitcase to take to school. When the final bell rang, her grandfather was waiting to take her to the country for the weekend. Their plantation provided every kind of adventure—fishing, helping in the garden, slopping the pigs, and playing with the new calves. She got puppy kisses and purrs from the dogs and cats that were around the house.

But more than anything, she was welcomed and adored by her grandparents and the people who worked for them. When her grandfather drove her back to school on Monday morning, her life with her family in town would begin for another week.

On the last day of school every year, she left town to stay with her grandparents for the entire summer. She never returned once to visit her parents and only moved back home at the last possible hour to enroll for the next year of school.

With her aunt's help, as soon as she graduated from high school, she ran as fast and as far away from her family as she could. Attending business school four hundred miles away, she thought everything in her past had been neatly swept under the rug. As far as she was concerned, her family no longer existed.

Many family members helped my mother avoid being at home, which makes me wonder how much they knew about what happened in her house. Whatever it was, until I wrote this book, it was never discussed.

My mother was a beautiful woman, but I don't think she ever felt beautiful or liked herself a single day of her life until she met my father. Handsome and athletic, he

whisked her off to football games, horse riding in the park, drinking parties, and fun. She thought this college boy with black curly hair and deep blue eyes was her ticket to lasting happiness.

In the months he courted her, he doted on her completely. He was crazy about her, and his attention made her feel very special. As surely as the prince's kiss woke Sleeping Beauty, my father's kiss gave an unhappy young woman hope for a different life. She thought the fairy tale would never end.

In the beginning, it looked like her dreams had come true. Her husband had plenty of free time for her as he only went to class a few hours a day. His numerous siblings and extended family provided fun activities and the warmth she had missed in her own family. Her "prince" escorted her on shopping trips to buy new furniture for their apartment. When he even helped hang curtains and install towel racks, she realized he could and would do almost anything she needed. She thought the bliss would never end. She had found heaven on earth.

With her husband by her side, her former shyness seemed to vanish. A funny, fun-loving young woman bubbled up. The cloud of depression that hung over her  throughout childhood disappeared in the glow of his attention and affection. Feeling safe and loved in the home they created, there wasn't a cloud on the horizon.

After their first year of marriage, he quit school to launch a new car agency with his brothers. The men worked long hours from sunrise to past sundown. When he finally came home in the evening, he was physically tired. All he wanted was a hello kiss from an adoring, grateful wife, an appreciative listening audience, and a hot meal on the table.

Shortly after dinner, he either went to a ballgame or listened to the plays over the radio. Some nights, he left with buddies for some local event. She began to feel unimportant and abandoned. Old insecurities from childhood plagued her.

She tried to tell him she felt abandoned when he worked late or went out at night, but he was too puzzled by her sudden insecurity to understand what she was saying. At first, he tried to be sympathetic: "Now baby, you know I love you. Don't be silly. I'm working hard for us so we can have a house and all the things we want." He would hold her close, she would calm down, and he thought all was well.

In the 1930s, most men got married, went to work, and came home to a warm meal on the table. Social life in small towns consisted of visiting friends and family you had known all your life. The intensity of those early days of marriage would naturally wane. He didn't depend solely on her for his happiness, contentment, or sense of accomplishment.

He didn't realize that she expected him to continue meeting her every need, that he was her emotional life raft. He was bewildered and troubled with her change into this fearful, needy woman.

It had been difficult enough for her when he began working long hours. If he left to fight in the war, her happiness would go with him. And what if her knight in shining armor fell on the battlefield? Her life would be over too. Her fears were so great, they overwhelmed any attempt she made to stay calm and rational.

This husband wasn't prepared for his young wife's behavior. For days she withdrew, never coming out of her room. He could hear her weeping, but suddenly, she would come out in a rage, spewing words he'd never heard from her mouth before. One minute she coldly and silently served him supper, and in the next minute, she desperately clung to him. As she grew more frightened, he grew more frustrated.

"What on God's green earth is wrong with you? You have a husband who loves you. You can buy whatever you want. You're a grown woman. Stop being a child. Make some friends. Visit my sisters. I don't care what you do, but stop blaming me. I don't know who you are anymore. For God's sake, woman, there's a war on."

She couldn't make friends or reach out to his sisters for help, because talking to them would reveal that she was insecure and unhappy with the brother they all loved. She kept her feelings hidden from everyone but her husband. She didn't realize she was alienating herself from the very people who would have offered support. She withdrew into herself more and more, afraid she would blurt something out. She used her time to methodically clean the house, cook, and bake.

Even to a sympathetic person, I don't think my mother could have explained the intensity of her feelings. She had never faced the hidden demons in her past. Growing up in a family tense with secrets and unresolved issues, she brought her wounds into the marriage. Unaware of what was caused her insecurity and anxiety, she continued to place the blame squarely on her husband's decision to go to war and leave her.

The pregnancy scheme had failed to keep her husband with her. Now she was stuck with this child, whether he came back or not. Trapped in a situation she didn't want, she began to mentally retreat. She couldn't face a reality in which she saw no way out.

My mother's oldest sister came to assist her for a couple of weeks immediately after I was born. My aunt joked good-naturedly when my mother quipped that I was the ugliest baby she had ever seen. (Interestingly, I am a carbon copy of my father's baby pictures.) But when she observed how my crying agitated my mother, she didn't laugh.

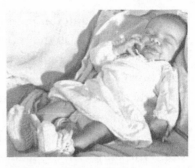

She was concerned as she watched my mother stand by the crib, holding a bottle to my mouth rather than nestling me close to feed me. The nursery rocking chair sat empty. In the forties, mothers were expected to be crazy about their infants. Something was terribly wrong with her sister, but what had happened?

My name was still Baby Girl, just as it had been on the birth certificate. Three different boy's monikers had been discussed by my parents, but no female names. Obviously, my mother thought a boy would be more desirable to my father. When my aunt (and indeed others) encouraged my mother to finally name me, I received my aunt's name. That name would always remind me that it was she who nurtured me at my birth. It is a name I finally came to understand over fifty years later.

My mother's family found out my father was being sent overseas and stepped in to rescue me. My mother needed help, and they gave her no choice but to move back to the home she had so wanted to leave. I know my father must have been relieved. As he watched his wife disappear into a world of her own, he was never sure what would happen next.

She dreaded returning to her childhood home, but it was a good move for me. Once we arrived, her three childless sisters swooped in like a small army of Mary Poppins to lovingly care for my infant needs. My mother may not have wanted me, but her sisters thought I was the most adorable child who had ever been born.

Early one morning, my aunts heard wailing from my mother's bedroom. They rushed in and found me on the floor, flailing and howling. I had fallen out of my mother's tall, four-poster bed. My mother lay motionless. They scooped me up and left the room, questioning one another: "How did this happen? Why was she just lying there, not checking to see if the baby was hurt? How had she fallen to the floor?"

My mother's mind was in another world, one in which she didn't have a baby. Today, we know her medical condition would be identified as severe postpartum depression, but no such information was available in the early 1940s. I was practically removed from her care.

Years later, she informed me that her family had restricted her to her room because of me and that she had no choice but to move back into that miserable house where she was criticized because of me. It makes sense that my mother resented me from the very beginning. For many years, I thought she hated me. Now I can see that she hated her situation.

I have grown to understand why my mother did everything she could to prevent having a child, knowing she could barely take care of herself. I would never have dreamed I would follow in her footsteps. I loved children almost as much as she avoided them.

My mother was trying to survive depression and rejection, while my aunts couldn't do enough to show me

I was loved. They buffered me as much as they could from the struggles beneath the surface of the family, and as the months and years passed, I blossomed into a pretty child with curly blonde hair and chubby cheeks. Sweet, candy-coated memories fill my mind of those loving days living with my affectionate aunts.

From the outside, no one would ever suspect the turmoil within the family. Everyone kept on a happy face, especially me.

2

Shame on You

Why was I ever born?
Jeremiah 20:18

My youngest aunt—only thirteen years older than I—was
my big sister, little mother, babysitter, and best friend all
rolled into one. I called her My T. I thought she was all
mine. My crib was moved into her room after I fell out of
my mother's bed, and this young aunt was the one who
changed my diaper and held me while I gulped down my
bottle in the middle of the night.

Once I started walking, I got into everything. My aunts
became so frustrated they found an old wooden playpen
to corral me—a small,
square structure with
slats that felt like jail
bars. I didn't like being
so restricted, and I am
told I made quite the
fuss.

Everyone was
relieved when My T
got home from school

12

and released me from my prison.

Many childhood photos display the sheer joy I shared with her. Whether she was holding my hand during my first hesitant steps, spraying me with the water hose, riding me on the handlebars, or making funny faces. In every photo, both of us are delighted and laughing. As I grew older, she took me everywhere. She always had an adventure in mind.

Once, she piled some neighborhood kids and me onto the old family mule. When that mule took off down the

road, we were barely hanging on. Screaming and laughing at the same time, we held on to anything we could. It may have been those screams that alerted my grandmother to our escapade, because she suddenly appeared right beside us in the farm truck. She never spoke a word, but the stern look on her face said it all. I dismounted and was driven home in steely silence.

About a week later, I was playing in the front yard. It was a perfect day to be outside. The sun was warm on my shoulders, and soft, fresh grass tickled my bare feet. I was a happy little girl. My T was reclining nearby in a faded striped-fabric lawn chair, the kind where your bottom almost touches the ground. Sipping a glass of cold sweet tea, she watched me exuberantly run around with one of Grandfather's prized round-bellied coonhound puppies following my every step.

Something called her into the house, probably for only seconds.

Enjoying my freedom, I sprinted across the street, with the puppy following close behind me. No sooner had I made it to the other side of the road when the screech of brakes and tires startled me.

I spun around and saw an unrecognizable bloody mess on the pavement right at my feet. I couldn't make sense of what had happened, but another aunt's screaming snapped me to attention. "Oh, my God. Oh, my God! What were you thinking? Look what you've done." She was yelling at My T, who was running toward me, but her words penetrated deeply.

Look what you've done! Look what you've done!

Those words would reverberate in my brain for years. It was my fault the puppy was dead in the street. I had done a terrible thing. I was devastated and frightened and began to cry. My usually affectionate aunt didn't comfort me. Instead, she told me to "stop it!"

Her abruptness was further proof that I had done something terribly wrong, and I better be quiet or I would be in even more trouble. In retrospect, I'm sure she was dreading how Grandfather was going to react to the death of his fine puppy and to the irresponsibility of the adults who didn't protect his only grandchild. If I had been hysterical, he would be even angrier.

Until that day, I had been tucked into a warm cocoon of childhood protection where bad things didn't happen. The puppy's death was only the first of several more disquieting events that would affect me for a lifetime.

Although I lived with my grandparents, I didn't have much interaction with them. They were locked in a war that kept them separate, spitting, or silent-married but living separately in the same house.

My grandfather, too old and sick to go to war, spent his days and nights alone in his bedroom, smoking pack after pack of Chesterfield cigarettes and taking an occasional swig of whiskey straight from the bottle. He lived in a house full of women and every one of them passed by his bedroom door without a glance in his direction. He lay on his bed, surrounded by a cloud of smoke and silence, watching people pass by his room as if he didn't exist. The reason the women treated him this way would remain hidden in the dark for much of my life.

My grandmother slept out on the "sleeping porch" every night, even in the freezing cold. She had her own bottle—the bottles of Coca-Cola she drank one after another. I remember the wooden box under the wall-fastened bottle opener—always spilling over with the bottle caps. When Coca-Cola was invented, cocaine was a legal ingredient in medicine, including the delicious new soft drink. At that time, no one realized the drug's potential harm, and I believe it was her addiction, helping her stay silent and cope with her despair.

It would be many years before I would understand why the women in the house shunned my grandfather. I thought he was great, always smiling and winking at me.

15

Sometimes when the adults were busy with their chores, I happily toddled into my grandfather's bedroom. Always glad to see me, he pulled me up to snuggle with him in his big green-leather rocking chair, but he never let me stay for long. He soon sent me on my way.

I was repeatedly told, in no uncertain terms, "Never go into your grandfather's bedroom." But how could I resist his ready affection and the can of King Leo peppermint sticks on the table right by his bed? One day, I sneaked into his room and was happily eating one of those peppermint sticks when my grandmother passed by the open door. She saw me standing close to him and jerked me out of his room so fast I was momentarily airborne.

She bent down close to my face and interrogated me. "What were you doing in there? What was your grandfather doing? I told you to stay out. Why did you disobey me?" I never had a chance to answer. She held me by both arms and shook me. "You're a bad, bad girl. Don't ever let me catch you with him again."

I was more emotionally stunned than physically harmed. Once again, my young mind drew the conclusion that I had done something terribly wrong. I didn't know exactly what it was, but there was no doubt that my grandmother found me guilty of a severe crime that required punishment. And I agreed.

Thinking I was at fault for the tension in the house, I judged myself harshly. For decades, I continued to sentence myself for taking the blame for everyone's unhappiness.

Even though I was nurtured by my aunts, in the shame of self-blame, I bit my fingernails into the quick and even scratched myself. Hurting myself seemed to give me relief from the guilt and shame.

During this time, I realized that food could calm me. I remember hiding in the closet and gobbling down sweets and salty chips as fast as I could get it into my mouth. But the relief was always temporary. Certain foods do contain mood-altering qualities, but I would struggle for years before I realized that no amount of food would be enough to make things better. Recovery from compulsive overeating became a lifelong struggle.

Depression, rage, overeating, alcoholism, and suicide riddled the lives of my mother and her brothers and sisters. I conclude that I wasn't the first child in the family to be exposed to my grandfather's inappropriate behavior or my grandmother's toxic hatred. The victims were left to figure it out on their own. But I get ahead of myself.

3
New Home

*Turn to me and have mercy, for I am alone
and in deep distress.*
Psalm 25:16

Almost three years had passed. One warm summer day in 1946, the repeated *aroooga* of a car horn was easy to hear through the open windows of my grandparents' home. When a car pulled into the driveway, the whole family rushed down the front steps to greet the driver. I trailed right behind them.

I didn't remember the man coming toward the house, but he knelt down and opened his arms wide the minute he saw me. Like iron to a magnet, I ran into his warm embrace. This man, returning from World War II, was my father. Quickly he went back to his car and brought out a large straw hat from the Philippines. I have no idea how he got it home, but I thought it was terrific and enjoyed running around to show it off.

We all sat around the big dining room table for lunch, and afterward, my father began loading many suitcases and boxes into his car. I didn't realize what was happening when he carried me to his car, and we drove away. I have a vague memory of looking out the long narrow rear window of his 1943 Chevy coupe's back seat. The people I loved grew smaller and smaller. Frightened and confused, I started to cry as my parents drove me away from the only family I had ever known.

My father pulled the car off the road to dry my tears and reassure me. From the moment he opened his arms to me in front of my grandparents' house, he became my knight in shining armor. I had no idea how significantly his warmth and affection would affect my mother for the rest of my life. He belonged to her, and I was an intruder into the magic and security she felt with him before I existed. She longed to rekindle the dream of what they once had together. How could he lavish so much of his attention on me? Didn't he realize how it made her feel?

We moved into an older neighborhood where mature trees towered over the rooftops. The exterior of our traditional house appeared peaceful to the neighbors driving by. In true southern tradition, everyone smiled and waved at the woman and little girl playing in the flower-filled front yard. They would have been shocked to know what went on inside that house.

When my father was out of the house and I went to my

mother for comfort or actual needs, I was frequently met with hurtful words. "What do you want? You always want something. God, you're driving me crazy. I wish you had never been born."

What had I done to make her hate me so? I wasn't old enough to understand the why, but I knew in every cell of my body that she didn't want me there. Her rejection left an emotional wound throbbing with pain that would send me searching to the ends of the earth for love to mend my broken heart.

I wanted to run so far away she could never find me, but running to my bedroom was about as far as I could go. Although my father's sister lived right across the street, my mother wouldn't allow me to visit. I wasn't able to run to her as my mother had in her childhood. I think she was afraid I would reveal something to my father's family. Behind the closed door, I learned to pretend my mother didn't exist.

What did I have to distract me from the anticipation of my mother's anger? Television and computers did not exist. Reading took me to other places, and I created relationships with fictional characters in my mind. My stuffed animals and plastic horses became my friends and family, and our "conversations" soothed my anxiety.

As I read about happy families, my imagination created magical possibilities. *If I could be a better kid, a good kid like in the books I read, maybe my mother would warm up to me.* I tried to change, but I could never be good enough for her to like me. I concluded, she saw something fundamentally unlovable about me. If a warm relationship with my mother depended on me, it was never going to happen.

I had been getting love and kisses from animals since I was old enough to walk. They were my friends and always had time to listen to my troubles. When something happened to any animal, it broke my heart.

In the fourth grade, I read Anna Sewell's book, *Black Beauty*. It was the story of a colt raised by a loving family. But after he was sold, he experienced abusive and neglectful situations. The horse never lost his good nature and faithfully gave his very best

to each owner, no matter how they treated him. In one season of his life, he was routinely whipped and worked to exhaustion under the weight of overloaded wagons. When he broke down physically and was of no use to them, the greedy owners sold him off like trash.

I was devastated by this book's truth: mean, cruel people exist, and others will stand by and do nothing to help the animals from being abused. I realized that good behavior doesn't prevent bad things from happening. Those were complicated concepts for a child to accept, but their reality fostered an underlying pessimism and depression about life.

Although Beauty finally canters to a happy ending, I sobbed uncontrollably every time I thought of this horse. A deep hatred of the kind of people who hurt Beauty began to seethe in my heart, and I made a sacred vow: *When I grow up, I will never stand by and see a helpless animal*

21

abused without trying to stop the perpetrator. Somehow, I would rescue any animal in need.

I never dreamed that I would feel some of that rage toward my own father.

When someone threw a puny cleft-palate puppy into the drainage ditch at the front of our property, I heroically resolved to save her. I held her shaking, whimpering little body close to me. No one thought the deformed puppy would live, but with the heart of Florence Nightingale and the patience of a saint, I spent hours bottle-feeding her. I thought I was saving her, but the warmth of her tiny body and the purpose she gave me actually helped save me. Together we celebrated each small victory, and her puppy kisses were a source of constant affection.

My mother never allowed that little dog in the house one time in her entire life. When it was freezing cold in the winter, I wanted to sleep in the garage and hold her for body warmth, but that wasn't allowed. Seeing my distress, my father found a small doghouse and put a lightbulb in it to help keep her warm. That sweet dog was my companion for twelve years. When I lost her, I thought I would never recover. She was my first baby.

4
Judgment

If we deliberately continue sinning after we have received knowledge of the truth, there is no longer any sacrifice that will cover these sins . . . only the terrible expectation of God's judgment and the raging fire.
Hebrews 10:26–27

I loved my father's family, especially his mother. She was the best of the best, about as round as she was tall. She always smelled like cookies. Her favorite things in the world were to attend church and cook for those she loved, in that order. I can still taste her fluffy white coconut cakes, warm buttery yeast rolls, and creamy homemade custard.

She was the happiest person I knew, and she often told me that her joy came from being loved by Jesus. One Saturday, when I was about four years old, she said that she and Papa were taking me to church.

I was thrilled. Would I finally get to meet this Jesus?

The Early Years

All dressed up in my best
sandals, a puffed-sleeve dress, and
lace-trimmed bonnet (all in pure
white), I was ready for my first
church visit.

Some church "sister" had
pulled brilliant orange-and-yellow
daylilies from her yard that
morning to decorate the church
altar. The pleasing fragrance of
those flowers wafted out to greet
us as we walked up the steps into
the church building. The stained-
glass windows cast hues of many
colors around the sanctuary. The
singing lifted me right up toward Heaven. I was
spellbound, every one of my senses stimulated.

After the songs, a tall dignified man solemnly rose
from a high-back chair on stage. He raised a tattered black
book high in the air. After a poignant moment of silence,
he sternly spoke. "This is the Good Book. This book is
about right and wrong, good and bad. And *you* better
choose right."

He bowed his head and earnestly pleaded with God to
keep the congregation from sinning and for the blood of
Jesus to save them all from hellfire. He mentioned good
works and lost sheep. I wondered about the sheep and the
blood when suddenly the man slammed his hand down on
the lectern so loudly that it startled me.

He spoke in a thunderous voice, and what I heard
frightened this bad little girl. He spoke with such authority
that I didn't doubt a word he said. His message was bad
news: God hated filth. And when we sinned, we became
filthy rags that disgusted God. He warned us that if we

24

didn't stop sinning, God would throw us into hellfire where we would burn alive forever. I was shaking as I huddled as close to my grandmother as possible.

When he pointed his finger at the congregation, sternly addressing us as, "You sinners," I felt like Almighty God himself was talking straight to me. How did the preacher know I was a filthy, disgusting little girl? My mother frequently condemned me with those very words in private, but it was something else to feel exposed to the whole congregation. Now I had another name to define myself. That name was *sin*, and I was a sinner.

Observing my nervousness after church, Grandma Susie explained that I didn't need to worry. Every single person is a sinner, a dirty old rag now and then. "Even me and Papa," she said. "But when you act good, God forgives your sins, and you are as white as snow—as white as your pretty dress."

Her explanation didn't make me feel better, because she didn't seem to know how bad I really was. I might look snow-white on the outside, but I was filled with dirty sin on the inside. Little girls who make their mothers unhappy must be terrible sinners, right? And I couldn't change myself enough to make my mother happy, no matter how hard I tried.

I was traumatized by my church visit. Terrorized by an image of burning in Hell forever, I was afraid to shut my eyes that night. The preacher's words and manner made a lasting impression on me. God's imminent judgment and eternal punishment in Hell stalked me, creating insomnia and morbid spine-chilling nightmares. When I finally did go to sleep, I might be startled awake, gasping for air and whimpering in fear and dread.

Even though I didn't go back to my grandparents' church, I heard plenty of good-works admonitions and sin talk from my relatives. I learned enough to know I had better pray hard for this filthy, bad girl to be forgiven.

I prayed from guilt and I prayed from fear. I earnestly bargained with God nightly: "If you forgive me for what I have done up to now, I'll never do it again." I meant it wholeheartedly.

The next morning, despite my promise to God, I would do something that made my mother furious. She would tell me once again, "You're driving me crazy."

I was never going to be acceptable to my mother and probably not to God either. *I must be such a disappointment to them both.* When a new sin showed its ugly face, I thought, *Maybe I have given up on trying to be good.* Next to lying to God, it was probably the worst sin. Maybe it was even a criminal act.

I hated my mother. Even my prayers expressed hateful thoughts about her. I prayed the police would come and put her in jail. I prayed someone would kidnap me, and maybe she would be sorry and be glad to get me back. I prayed my father would divorce her and marry me. God couldn't have liked that prayer, and I heaped more guilt and fear on myself. Then I confessed and begged for forgiveness.

Someone else was always praying for forgiveness too. I have never known a more devout Christian than my grandmother. I believe she tried every minute of her life to follow everything the Good Book said. Morbidly obese and almost blind, this kind, loving woman, who loved Jesus more than anyone I had ever known, lived out her last days in a nursing home, fearing she hadn't been good enough to earn her way into Heaven. She suffered from the same fear created by the "filthy rag preaching" that scared me as a young child. When I saw my grandmother weep in fear, I hated God for what he was doing to her, never realizing that it was the preacher who spoke those frightful, condemning words, not God.

5

Daddy

*The Lord is slow to anger and filled with
unfailing love, forgiving every kind of sin and
rebellion. But he does not excuse the guilty.
He lays the sins of the parents upon their
children; the entire family is affected.*
Numbers 14:18

An innocuous black-and-white snapshot reveals clues to a
critical part of my story. The photo shows a Clark-Gable-
handsome soldier holding a baby
girl astride a big chestnut mare.
The soldier in that photo is my
daddy, and I am the little girl
seated for my first "ride" at five
months. This photo foretells the
unfolding of the next fifteen years
when nothing would compare to
horses and my daddy. Two days
later, this handsome soldier left his wife and child to serve
with US troops in the Philippine Islands.

When he returned from the war, he purchased the first
of many horses he would buy for me. Dolly the Great, we

28

named her. A shaggy Shetland, short and stout, she was just the right height for me to bury my cheek in the

 blanket of her soft coat. Leaning against her belly, I began to have a soothing attachment to animals that lasts to this day. When I connected with Dolly and Baby, they helped dry the tears I cried over my mother's rejection.

At sunset each night, I sat on the back steps of our house, waiting for my lack of parental affection to end. When my father stepped out of his car, my world changed. His touch made me feel wanted. I was hungry for love and touch, and I was too young to realize how my mother felt about our closeness. I innocently received all the affection Daddy had to give.

By the time I entered first grade, my father and I spent more and more time together as he taught me to ride. My grandfather was a renowned horseman in his day, and my father saddled up right behind him. Now it was my turn to put my feet into the stirrups and carry on the family name.

My grandfather picked me up every afternoon in his big-finned Cadillac and drove me to his farm to practice my riding. Seated by the oval track, he propped his abscessed leg up on a metal water bucket, placed his hand on top of his walking cane, and sat like a monarch watching over his dynasty. He was there to oversee his son coach the little princess in how to mount the big horses. There would be no more Shetland ponies for this six-year-old. I was ready to enter the world of competitive horse shows.

I spent every possible moment I could enjoying my daddy's coaching and admiration. What little girl wouldn't love being the apple of her father's eye? I didn't know I was missing activities that are important for girls. I didn't attend slumber parties or learn to roller skate with friends my age, because I went to the farm every day, seven days a week. The other kids seemed like such babies to me. I couldn't wait until the school bell rang so I could be back in my father's world.

I relished this grown man's attention and felt very lucky. I was becoming well known in the horse show world, even though I was one of the youngest competitors. When hundreds of people rose to their feet and cheered as I entered the arena, I was exhilarated. My daddy was the one who made it all happen, and I was "over the moon" for him. Missing a few childish birthday parties seemed totally unimportant.

When things went the way my father wanted them, he was popular and fun. When things didn't go his way, all hell broke loose. With curses flying out of his mouth and fists ready to punch anyone who made him angry, my father could go shockingly, momentarily crazy. His hair-trigger temper could erupt toward anything and anybody—man, beast, or inanimate object. Once, he hit his car with a hammer because it wouldn't start.

He was a true Jekyll and Hyde. He was usually outgoing and generous, but his entire personality could change in a split second. All the applause in the world couldn't make up for those times when my doting, affectionate father terrified me with his rage. Witnessing these out-of-control episodes, I must have wondered, *Would he ever get this mad at me?* But his affection was so needed, I had to deny the possibility.

His rage toward people frightened me, but I could hardly endure his anger toward animals. Firmly grounded in my vow to prevent abuse, I faced a challenging dilemma. When a young horse reared and fell backward, breaking the long shaft of the expensive cart my father was driving, Daddy started whipping her with the long leather reins. I became hysterical. I rushed at him, crying and screaming, "No! No! No! Stop! Are you insane?" If our groom hadn't intervened and stopped me from reaching him, I don't know what would have happened.

I had to take some kind of action to punish my father's cruelty. Despite the possible consequences, I took a sharp knife and cut his expensive new whip into small pieces. It was a daring move, and I felt brave and strong.

For the first and only time in my life, he used the pieces of that whip to switch me. I didn't care. That little act of revenge was worth it. No one was going to mistreat an animal on my watch, not even him.

Knowing an explosion could go off at any moment, we all got up every morning and went about life as if nothing unusual was happening. Daily I sat quietly in my elementary school classes, fearing what would happen if I told anyone about what happened in my house. Abuse was permitted, but talking about it was forbidden.

It's a wonder I learned anything at all in school. I was so preoccupied hiding my angst and keeping secrets that I was in a constant state of anxiety and depression.

But I felt safe at school, and the distraction of the lessons helped me stuff everything that was happening at home into a lockbox of denial. I temporarily escaped reality and perfected the art of appearing calm outside while hanging by a thread on the inside. But in the night, my defense mechanisms disappeared, and violent, terrifying nightmares frequently startled me awake.

6

Danger

The Lord keeps watch over you as you
come and go, both now and forever.
Psalm 121:8

Nothing made my father happier than the atmosphere of a county fair. The stable smells of fresh straw, horses, and saddle leather were heavenly to him. It was his world, and I loved all the things he loved.

When I was five until I was fifteen, I traveled all summer with my father as we followed the horse show circuit. Everywhere we went, we were a winning pair. Despite episodes when my father drank too much or his temper got the best of him, my life felt complete when we were together.

We ate our meals together, dressed for the evening's competition, listened to "Rock Around the Clock" on the radio, and danced together at

33

parties. I felt like such a lucky girl. We were both getting something we wanted. I got the attention I craved. He got blind adoration and a willing student who only wanted to please him. I dreamed that the two of us would spend the rest of our lives together.

The more time I spent with my father, the more intensely my mother resented me. When he was away, she couldn't say enough cruel things to me or hit my backside hard enough with his belt. When I finally told my father how much she hated me and asked him to send me away to boarding school, I thought he would protect me. I thought he would at least put her in her place. Maybe my secret hopes would come true—he would divorce her and she would be the one sent away. But everything continued as it was.

This was my first realization that my father wasn't going to protect me from her or change our family structure. He did whatever he wanted and got what he wanted. His daughter adored him, and his wife took care of the house. From his perspective, things were working just fine.

My mother was suffering something no woman should have to endure in her marriage. Although I didn't understand it, she saw the situation correctly. Her husband preferred to spend his time with another female. It made no difference that the other female was her young daughter. Fearing he might choose me if she forced him to make a choice, I believe she decided she would wait it out until I was gone.

Mother may have seen my relationship with her husband as something she wanted for herself, but his attention to my welfare became almost nonexistent. Because of his own ego, he put me on horses beyond my ability to control. More than once, horses injured me as they ran through fences or reared and fell back on me.

When we arrived at the fairgrounds, Daddy and the grooms got the horses settled into their stalls and arranged the tack room. Simultaneously, the carnies were setting the midway rides, gaming booths, and their living spaces. Their trailer homes were often close to the horse barns.

I was left to roam the fairgrounds on my own. In every town, day laborers congregated around horse barns and carnivals, looking for a quick buck.

My daddy wouldn't have liked it at all if he'd known his pretty young daughter was wandering among the men setting up the midway. It wouldn't have taken a second for one of them to drag me behind a piece of equipment or into a trailer. In the confusion and noise, I doubt anyone would have heard me screaming. I was oblivious to the danger around me, because I thought the men who worked on the midway were my friends. I liked men. I lived in a man's world around the track.

Eventually, I got myself into a potentially disastrous situation. I was fascinated by the dark-skinned, exotically dressed crystal-gazing gypsies who traveled with the carnival. The women's laughing eyes beckoned others into their tents for palm readings. They were dressed in long colorful skirts and had dangling earrings. As they danced around the campfire, the coin belts wrapped around their hips jangled in the night. For a teenage girl whose mother didn't enjoy being a woman, these gals had a secret I wanted to know.

The fact that this gypsy tribe traveled with a real live prince was as romantic as a girl could hope for in her wildest teenage dreams. With an unruly shock of ebony black hair and multiple earrings, he made quite an impression. They seemed so friendly, but it's probably more accurate to say the fortune tellers were good at enticing people into their ornately decorated tent to pay the fee for whatever they saw in their crystal ball.

One sticky summer afternoon, I lazily sauntered over to their campsite. Rundown trailers, bubble-shaped campers, and elaborately carved carts sat in a wagon-train type circle. Men, women, and children milled about or sat around a small fire where they cooked their meals. One of the young Tarot card readers invited me into her stuffy trailer. A few minutes into our soiree, she casually looked out the open door and said, "They're talking about you." She indicated a tight-knit circle of men and women excitedly gesturing and talking all at once.

Her observation intrigued me. *They're talking about me?*

She didn't answer, but smiled coyly.

The oldest woman in the camp approached the trailer and entered to announce some exciting news. "My darling girl, you've been chosen to marry the prince."

Did I hear her correctly? Marry? Prince? I had been chosen to marry the prince? Would I be a princess? For someone who has felt rejected, *chosen* is a precious, powerful word. For a moment, it was the only word I heard. I didn't realize I was in real danger. I certainly didn't know that bride kidnapping is a common practice among the Romani gypsies in Europe. The reluctant bride was only returned to her frantic family when a ransom was paid.

On the last day of the fair, I went to say goodbye, and the family attempted to restrain me in their trailer. They were moving out, and I knew I needed to run. I wrenched out of their grip and sprinted so fast that I ran out of my shoes. I never went back for those shoes, and I certainly never told my father what had happened.

When the horse show ended late at night and the horses were cooled and stabled, I drove my father back to our home town. At age thirteen, I was speeding along narrow two-lane winding country roads in his big Lincoln Continental. I felt grown up, needed, and quite proud of myself. But to put a child behind the wheel of a two-ton lethal weapon is irresponsible and dangerous. Who was taking care of whom?

My father's good behavior was endearing. His words were a salve to the emotional rejection from my mother. As long as he was my sweet daddy, I was able to repress, deny, or at least minimize the possibility that he could suddenly lose his temper or that he was putting me in danger. Alcohol sometimes fueled his out-of-control behavior, and I think blackouts kept him from remembering his acts.

As a WWII veteran, my father was engaged in combat in the Philippine Islands. PTSD had not been identified when these men and women returned home and tried to resume their lives. Unless they were hopelessly insane, they were left to fend for themselves. I don't know if anyone, including my father, realized that he might still be on the battlefield fighting an unseen enemy. PTSD would explain his hair-trigger rage and need for alcohol to fight internal demons.

I rationalized his rage, because his violence wasn't directed at me and because I needed him for so many reasons. I could always hope it wouldn't happen again.

7
Hypocrites

Don't follow their example, for they don't practice what they teach. They crush people with unbearable religious demands and never lift a finger to ease the burden.
Matthew 23:3–4

When I was thirteen, my father moved beyond local city politics and became a candidate for county sheriff. His campaign manager suggested it would look good and increase his voter base if he attended church. The following Sunday morning, my father drove my mother and me to the oldest church with the tallest steeple in our town. While we marched down the center aisle, looking like the most functional family you have ever seen. My father shook hands left and right with people he had known most of his life. He was a hometown boy enjoying a campaign opportunity. In looking back, I wonder if he lost the election because some of these same people had witnessed his flashes of rage after returning from the war.

This city church was surprisingly less threatening than the one I attended with my grandparents at age four. There was no shouting about sin and Hell. In fact, there was no shouting at all, and I don't think I ever heard the word *Hell* mentioned. The parishioners were so friendly, greeting us like their long-lost friends every Sunday as we approached the massive wooden doors that opened into the sanctuary.

The church kids didn't seem to know I was different. Their friendliness and acceptance gave me a little breathing room from the damning thoughts I had about myself. A tiny spark of hope began to grow in this self-proclaimed sinful girl. Maybe I wasn't as bad as I thought.

That spark roared into an intense desire to pursue religion and become a first-class good girl. I observed others closely to see what made them good church-going folks. Almost everyone owned a Bible. Thick black Bibles were tucked under men's arms, and women used pretty little zippered cases to carry theirs. The first step I took was to buy a pure white Bible with a scripture-embossed carrying case. At least I was looking good.

I vowed to read my Bible from beginning to end. If I did what it said, maybe I could prevent my descent into that Hell I first heard about in my grandmother's church.

The first night of Bible ownership, warmly snuggled down in my bed, I started reading Genesis. In the third chapter, sin entered the narrative. I was no stranger to sin, and I began to grow apprehensive as I read.

By the sixth chapter, God was so disgusted with people that he regretted ever creating them. With a vast flood, he destroyed everything and everybody except for a few chosen people and animals. I doubted a girl like me would have been one of the chosen ones.

The Bible wasn't helping me comprehend how the Christians at church seemed so happy. No one knew how the Bible frightened me. I had no one at home to ask about the harshness of the Lord, and I didn't dare ask anyone at church for fear of revealing my ignorance and possibly condemning myself.

I got even better at hiding my fear and despair. I acted like I was just one of the smiling people attending church. I hoped that if I hung around long enough, I would discover how church people could seem so unconcerned when God's vengeance hung over their heads every minute. Evidently, they were as good inside as they appeared on the outside. I needed to try harder, and I needed a mission.

One Wednesday evening after the church potluck supper, a visiting missionary set up a rickety screen in the sanctuary. The click-click-click of film ran through a projector's metal spools. As the light flashed onto the screen, I saw ink-black children dancing joyfully in the dirt of an African village. At first, I didn't see the reason for their excitement, but the missionary said they had just heard "the good news about Jesus." Their faces were glowing, because they believed Jesus came from Heaven to love them and to save them. They would be blessed on Earth and go to Heaven when they died. Although nothing had changed in their extreme poverty, they laughed and danced as if nothing mattered other than knowing Jesus.

I didn't know their kind of joy. I longed to experience that comforting sense of trust, but I didn't know how to get it. I believed God existed, but that belief hadn't produced any peace. The only thing that made sense was that my sin blocked the light of God's love. I tried my best to follow the rules, but I failed over and over. I confessed and confessed, but I kept on sinning.

Maybe there was no hope for someone like me. I was feeling discouraged, but I kept on listening. The missionary read from 1 Peter in the Bible. If Scripture is God's Holy Word, I heard God say something about me that I had never heard before.

> *You are a chosen people. You are royal priests, a holy nation, God's very own possession. As a result, you can show others the goodness of God, for he called you out of the darkness into his wonderful light (1 Peter 2:9).*

I almost gasped. I was chosen? Royal? I belonged to God? I could show others the light? How?

I paid close attention to every word he said.

The second scripture gave me marching orders. I could go somewhere for God:

> *How can they call on him to save them unless they believe in him? And how can they believe in him if they have never heard about him? And how can they hear about him unless someone tells them? And how will anyone go and tell them without being sent? That is why the Scriptures say, "How beautiful are the feet of messengers who bring good news!" (Romans 10:14-15).*

I finally had an inkling of something I could do to please God. He wanted even a sinner like me to know I could serve him and be a messenger with the beautiful feet that made little children happy.

When the missionary asked people to come to the front of the room if they wanted to serve the lost, my feet moved me right to the front of the room. For the first time in my life, I felt sure God wanted me to do something for him. I was ready to go to the darkest place on Earth, because precious little children were going to Hell if somebody from the church didn't show up.

The missionary went on to say it was our job to invite people into the Kingdom. My interpretation? Invite people to church. He said we would meet people in our day-to-day life who didn't know Jesus. Right then and there, I decided I would do it. I would tell people about Jesus.

I was so happy, and I wanted to find somebody right away to save. Soon after I decided to be an Ambassador for God, I met a teenage boy from the other side of town. Buddy was the prototype for John Travolta's part in the movie *Grease*, which would be produced twenty years later. With his slicked-back 1950s-style greaser hair, a cigarette pack in his T-shirt pocket, and a black leather jacket, he was devilishly handsome. Only a year older than I was, he already looked like an adult.

As I engaged him in conversation, I got right to the point. "Where do you go to church?"

He was raised in the Catholic Church but no longer attended. I didn't even know what a Catholic was, but no matter, I had my first potential convert.

Lady Luck had surely brought this poor lost soul right to me. On the spot, I "spoke for Christ" and invited him to the Christmas Eve service at our church. He accepted. It was a Christmas miracle.

I waited in freezing cold weather in front of the church. My parents had already quit going to church, but they dropped me off for the service. I almost gave up on him, but finally I heard the sound of his motorbike in the quiet night. By the time we got inside, the only available seats were at the front of the candle-lit sanctuary. To the shock of the affluent parishioners, we made our grand entrance down the center aisle.

Within three days, my parents' phone had blown up with protests from my Sunday school teacher, youth group leader, and the minister's wife. My mother was so ashamed, she said, "We'll have to leave town." She convinced me that the whole congregation wanted to protect their pure, good children from me. I was uninvited to church. I was no longer welcome.

Deeply hurt, I wanted to defend myself, but to whom? What had I done wrong? I brought a lost soul to church. Isn't that what the missionary told all of us to do? Why couldn't they understand my missionary zeal? I was trying to be like Jesus.

If one person had come forward to counsel me, the next forty years of my life might have been very different. I needed help to understand the Gospel, but I received judgment and condemnation. I didn't understand church or Christians. They seemed like mean, self-righteous-bullies.

I wanted nothing more to do with God or anyone associated with him. The world was upside down—the supposedly good people were awful. Or maybe . . . there weren't any good people. I found consolation from other kids who didn't go to church. They thought church rhetoric was a bunch of silly propaganda and nothing to worry about. I learned to drink and smoke and do whatever would make me popular. I was as clean as the driven snow when I left the church, but it wouldn't be long before this girl, who had struggled to be good, would enjoy being bad.

Riding was as natural to me as breathing, and although it gave me great joy, this is one of the last photos taken of me on a horse. Other things became more important than my father and riding.

8

The Sixties

All of us used to live that way, following the
passionate desires and inclinations of our
sinful nature. By our very nature we were
subject to God's anger, just like everyone else.
Ephesians 2:3

By age fourteen, I appreciated the immediate calming effects of alcohol. It was easy to get into my father's liquor. With the first few sips, my oppressive anxiety and angst was lifted, replaced with light-heartedness. The word *sin* slid easily out of my vocabulary.

Alcohol eased my way into backseat romances. Being held by a boy satisfied my deep longing to be wanted, and gave me a temporary reprieve from loneliness. Holding on to a male was a fix I would use for many years. By now, my father was disgusted with my interest in boys. Without God or either parent who seemed to care, I felt untethered. I didn't know if I would ever land in a safe place.

After testing out of my junior year, I was only fifteen years old when I entered my senior year of high school. I was already acting well beyond my age when I met my first serious boyfriend—a twenty-year-old tall, blond college sophomore. With the Platters' singing "Smoke Gets in Your Eyes" in the background, he whisked me onto the dance floor and held me close all night. When the music stopped, I was a smitten kitten. If this was love, it was the best feeling in the world.

To really understand what that night was like for me, you would have to rent the 1951 version of the *Rainmaker*, starring a young, handsome, charismatic Burt Lancaster. Not only did my dance partner look like Burt Lancaster, he also carried the magic of the character *Starbuck* that night. I was his *Lizzie*. I had never felt so beautiful or so hopeful.

During the years we dated, his jealousy bewildered me. Head-over-heels for him, no one else could have captured my heart. There were break-ups and make-ups, apologies and tears, but our physical attraction for each other drew us back together. When I left for college, we got together as often as possible, but the distance became too difficult to sustain the passion. We met other people, and were not always on the same page, politically.

We were essentially out of each other's lives—almost. From time to time, one of us reached out to the other. Without fail, the magnetism was still there. When we met, it was as if no time had passed at all. We sometimes wondered aloud why we weren't together, but we moved on time and time again.

When I transferred to a co-ed college, I stepped right into the 1960s counter-culture of sex, drugs, and rock & roll. I don't know why the other students were so angry and discontented, but I had years of pent-up anger from childhood and rejection from the church. Many of us were time bombs just waiting for the right opportunity to explode against any kind of authority or repression.

Eastern religion had invaded college campuses, and many of us thought we were bound straight for nirvana. *dharma, karma, bliss,* and *guru* became buzzwords, as did *feminism, racism,* and *sexism.* Hoping the Kama Sutra and various drugs would provide a transcendental experience of higher consciousness, we ventured into some dangerous places. I thought I had found my spiritual path.

We wanted to change the world and right every wrong. Drawn toward any cause that demanded social change, we eagerly marched for the rights of minorities and women. When Governor Faubus used troops to thwart desegregation in Arkansas schools, I was so incensed that I wanted to get on a Freedom bus and head south.

Vietnam pulled boys I knew into military service and early death. We made banners reading MAKE LOVE, NOT WAR, BAN THE BOMB, and WAR IS NOT HEALTHY FOR CHILDREN AND OTHER LIVING THINGS. I think our hearts were in the right place, but our minds were not clear.

We grieved when JFK was assassinated. We had lost an influential leader who supported our causes. But nothing stopped us from rocking on into the night with the music of Chuck Berry and Little Richard blaring in the background. It was our way of trying to forget the crazy world around us for as long as possible.

Drugs and alcohol blunted our anxiety, masked our depression, and allowed us to have mindless fun. Those nights helped me forget anything I didn't want to remember and provided an escape from the doubts and fears that made me miserable. People were dying from contaminated drugs, but the relief I felt made me more than willing to take the chance.

I'm not sure how I attended enough classes to graduate from college. The only proof I have, besides a diploma, is a photo of me walking across a stage in a cap and gown. The actual experience is not in my memory bank.

The Trying Years

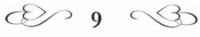

9

Agony and Ecstasy

What I always feared has happened to me.
What I dreaded has come true. I have no
peace, no quietness. I have no rest; only
trouble comes.
Job 3:25–26

Post-graduation, I realized you couldn't make a living with a BA in English, so I went back to school and became a dental hygienist. I didn't particularly want to be a hygienist, but I wanted a sure way to make a living so I could leave town and never look back. Once I passed my exams, I moved west with the hope I could start anew. I resolved to make better choices and lead a healthier life.

Moving to the extreme heat of a desert climate was definitely an adjustment. A simple chore like filling my car with gas left me drenched and wiped out. Gradually, I unpacked the many boxes that contained my belongings, and my apartment began to look like a home. The new job was demanding, and I could hardly wait for the weekends when I could sleep in, lie by the pool, and generally relax.

On an ordinary Saturday, I got my errands done early while it was still somewhat cool. I got an hour of sun, cleaned the apartment, and slipped into a skimpy baby-doll top to reward myself with a long afternoon nap in the cool of the air conditioning. No sooner had I gotten comfy in bed than the doorbell interrupted my rest.

Slightly irritated, I trudged barefoot to the front door. When I opened the door, that handsome high school boyfriend smiled at me with those perfect teeth and a mischievous grin. We hadn't spoken in over a year, but the same intense physical attraction I felt when he first whisked me onto the dance floor caused me to flush. It seemed like the most natural thing in the world for him to be standing there.

Neither of us spoke a word as he stepped inside the apartment, closing the door behind him. My heart was beating out of my chest. His eyes never left mine as he took my hand. Everything in the world disappeared but his face. He turned and led me into the bedroom.

In the afterglow of our sexual reunion, he casually said, "After all these years, you're the woman I can't get out of my mind. I know you feel the same way about me. Why don't we just give in, quit fooling around, and get married?"

Did he just propose? I wasn't entirely sure. I pulled away from his embrace and sat up in bed. "Are you serious?"

"I'm serious," he said.

Thoughts flew through my head. I'm twenty-four years old. Who or what was I hoping to find? We knew each other—the good, the bad, and the ugly. And yet, here we were together, and he wanted me.

It wasn't the most romantic proposal. It was almost an afterthought, and I was about to base my whole future on that one question. I knew the marriage might not turn out well, but what if it could? If we could work it out, I would have the family I had always wanted. If it didn't work out, we could close the door on the back-and-forth we'd danced for nine years.

And with those pragmatic thoughts, I said okay. My future husband returned home, and I started repacking. Like any soon-to-be-married couple, we made plans for our future. He would go to graduate school, and I would continue working. We looked forward to owning a home, getting a dog, and having children.

Our plans were nothing out of the ordinary, but we were not an ordinary couple. The night before we married, we had a loud shouting match, foretelling a volatile future. The yelling didn't stop us from driving to the state line the next morning and getting married in a quaint old courthouse.

My husband's gender expectations were not unusual for the times. Although the 1960s would eventually offer women more choices, most of us were stuck in the 1950s where women were supposed to look like Loretta Young sweeping through those double doors on her television show. We were told in so many ways that the role we were born to fulfill was wife and mother. Even though Lesley Gore's hit song "You Don't Own Me" climbed the charts, *Father knows Best* and *Leave it to Beaver* were the most popular shows we watched. Wives met their husband's needs and supported their goals and careers. I wanted to be a good wife.

While my husband attended graduate school, I worked, typed his papers, and learned to make his favorite southern delicacy—cornbread hushpuppies. It was sweet when he appreciated my cooking and support, but it wasn't enough to gratify my desire to shine and be recognized as having some abilities and intelligence. I was out of step with the times and didn't know how to productively change things. It seemed I was always fighting someone or something.

I resented that he could do whatever he wanted during the day while I worked to support us financially. It was one thing when he left for night class, but when he began spending entire nights studying at the library, I felt alone and rejected. Unfortunately, the quiet desperation of my loneliness didn't stay silent.

I complained and begged for more attention. In my husband's eyes, my needs were childish, undesirable, and unwanted. He was irritated and said he needed a "grown-up" woman to further his career. I think it shocked us both that my anger got out-of-control so quickly. I didn't know I was unconsciously fighting the father who had controlled me, a society that held me back, and a husband who belittled me.

I take the blame for many of our fights. My defiance and pent-up anger escalated me into a crazed woman. At the same time, my husband's anger and lack of patience were escalating too. When our hot tempers flared, we spewed ugly threats and used physical force against each other. We were either in honeymoon heaven or fighting like hell. Make-up sex smoothed everything over—until the next time.

Time after time, I thought about leaving, but no matter how bad things got, when he pulled me onto his lap and called me his baby, I never wanted to go. No drug produced the same soothing connection and contentment I felt nestled against his chest. Maternal deprivation had left me with a hunger for skin contact. I tried to quench that longing in the arms of a man.

Those moments in his lap blocked out anything that had happened only moments before. In the perceived safety of his embrace, my emptiness filled, my longing quieted, I stayed in the marriage.

Those euphoric moments became few and far between. My husband was leaving, physically and emotionally. Fear of abandonment gripped my heart. The more I tried to get reassurance, the more I repulsed him.

"You better get it together and act like a grownup woman," he said.

I couldn't. I couldn't get myself together, but I couldn't give up trying to get this man to love me, either. I was locked in a hopeless battle.

One night at dinner, he casually delivered the final blow. "I'm sick and tired of your tears and insecurity. I'm bored with this relationship. I told you to grow up. I need a woman, a partner. I don't know why I was ever attracted to you. I'm done. You'll be served with divorce papers when I get around to it. In the meantime, leave me alone, and don't expect me to act married."

His words hurt me, but somehow they didn't crush me. I guess I went numb with denial. But what he said next confirmed my worst fear. "You're a child, a plaything, and no grown man is ever going to put up with your foolish immaturity. Stop acting like such a baby."

He was right. My neediness was disgusting.

A scene from the movie *A Streetcar Named Desire* flashed through my mind. Blanche Dubois was being led away to a mental institution. She looked up at the doctor escorting her and said, "I have always depended on the kindness of strangers." I knew my life might well end up like hers—depending on strangers because no one wanted me.

When my husband walked out our front door without looking back, I wanted to stop living. I wanted to stop hurting. I rather calmly decided I would rather die than live alone and unloved.

I sat down with my monogrammed wedding stationery and dipped my husband's wedding gift, an expensive Montblanc fountain pen, into a glass bottle of black ink. I wrote two words: *I'm sorry.* I was sorry for a thousand things, but those two words said it all. I stopped writing. There was nothing else to say. And no one else to write. Who cared?

Like a person sleepwalking, I took a long, hot shower. With shaking hands, I made up my face and put on my brightest lipstick. After slipping into a lovely gown from my trousseau, I swallowed an entire bottle of potent sleeping pills and lay down on our freshly made bed.

I don't remember thinking about what my husband would do when he found me. I guess part of me wished he would fall apart by the bedside, sorrowful and repentant, regretting that he threw me away. I don't know what he did. I was nearly dead when he found me.

The next thing I knew, someone was pushing a tube down my nose, and I was gagging. Thirty hours later, I woke up in a hospital room with a nurse guarding me to prevent any further attempts to hurt myself. I was furious that I didn't escape my lonely life.

During post-suicide psychiatric treatment, an unscrupulous young intern told my husband that with the severity of my depression, I would probably succeed in killing myself one day.

I believe that information was pivotal in his decision to divorce me. And the doctor was almost right. It wouldn't be the last time I wanted to die..

↬ 10 ↫
Loss after Loss

*I knew you before I formed you
in your mother's womb.
Jeremiah 1:5*

I was living apart from my soon-to-be ex-husband when I
discovered I was pregnant. Intermittently, between the
fights and the begging, we had continued having "make-up
sex." My emotions ricocheted from one extreme to the
other. If I told him I was pregnant, he would probably say
all the right words, even take me into his arms. But if I
displeased him, he would fault me for being a *poor excuse for
a wife* and brand me as a *bad mother*.

If I stayed married and then we divorced, the courts
would probably give custody of my child to him and his
parents. My family would not want the child or help me.
The potent medications I took to keep my demons at bay
might have hurt the fetus. Many thoughts went through
my mind, but the deciding factor was the fear that I
wouldn't be a good mother. If I treated a child like my
mother abused me, I surely couldn't live with myself.

I had to make a decision and soon. In the end, I
convinced myself that a child would be better off never

being born than to have me for a mother. Abortion seemed like the only solution.

I asked my psychiatrist what he thought. He said, "You can't take care of yourself. How are you going to take care of a baby?" His observation was the nail in the coffin of my pregnancy, but I don't blame him. There was truth in what he said.

Abortion was illegal and extremely dangerous. It took many phone calls and dead alleys before I finally got a phone number that paid off. The female voice on the other end of the line gruffly said, "Bring cash. Come alone, and come after midnight."

At 1:00 a.m., I drove myself to a part of town I'd never ventured into before. I pulled into the dark, rundown trailer park and found the address that the voice had given me. Tall weeds almost prevented me from reaching the door of a single-wide. I couldn't imagine that anyone lived here. When I knocked on the paint-peeling door, a giant black dog chained at the side of the trailer started snarling and barking.

An arm reached out and jerked me inside. "Get in here, stupid. You want the whole town to know what's going on?"

The gruff voice belonged to a female whose facial makeup was so outlandish I was startled. Orange-red frizzy hair was teased to the tip of each strand while dark red circles of rouge adorned her cheeks. Neon-orange lipstick gave her the appearance of a clown about to jump into a circus ring. Could she be the person about to perform the abortion?

Where was the doctor?

She demanded the cash and then impatiently pushed me into a cramped bathroom. "Get on the floor and put your legs over the side of the tub." A straightened-out coat hanger was lying in the bathtub. The floor was dirty, and the stench almost made me retch. I felt as filthy as my surroundings.

While swearing at the dog to stop barking, she stepped into the tub and ordered me to spread my legs. I couldn't see what she was doing from my position on the floor, but there was a sharp pain as she pushed something far inside me. Surely she didn't use the coat hanger. She stepped out of the tub, pulled me up, and almost shoved me out the door. I staggered into the night, nauseous and weeping.

The procedure should have resulted in expelling the fetus within forty-eight hours. Those were long hours. I was alone in my apartment, and no one knew what I had done. I was cramping and spotting, but nothing else happened.

Days went by. I changed my mind every few hours. I thought I felt the baby move. *That's impossible*, I told myself. It was a tiny blob, certainly not big enough for me to feel movement.

My thoughts went from one horrifying extreme to another. *I've made a terrible mistake. Is there any way to go back? Should I pull the abortion apparatus out? If I did that and the procedure had maimed the child, would it be born deformed?* The crushing guilt and uncertainty about what to do almost drove me to kill us both.

Instead, I did the unthinkable. I went back to that same dirty, smelly trailer so the clown lady could complete her job.

During this visit, the vicious black dog was tied up at the front doorsteps, baring his teeth and growling down low from his broad chest. His head was as big as a watermelon. I'd never met an animal I didn't think I could win over, but this dog was so obviously dangerous, he gave me a chill.

A heavyset man came around the side of the trailer and pulled the dog aside so I could get past. The dog continued barking furiously the entire time I was in the trailer. It made the woman nervous, and she rushed through a more grueling procedure. She told me never to come back.

More days passed. Suddenly, the supposedly simple abortion turned into a nightmare of heavy bleeding and intense uterine contractions. Even though I knew I might die from blood loss, I was afraid to call anyone. Abortion was illegal. I was committing a crime.

Finally, the intensity of the pain became unbearable. I had to get help. My husband was the last person on earth I wanted to know about the abortion, but he lived close by and I was desperate.

He came immediately after I called and found me on the bathroom floor. The blood and my condition shocked him. He helped me up, grabbed what towels were still dry and got me to his car.

While driving at top speed to the nearest hospital, he questioned me about what was happening. Sobbing, I told him what I had done. His concern turned to cold contempt. "You killed my baby?" He said it several times as if he couldn't grasp the truth of it. I think he wanted to dump me in the street.

When we arrived at a Baptist hospital, I could only imagine the disdain the pious Christian nurses and doctors had for me. I was a murderer and a criminal. Maybe they compassionately saw a desperate young woman, but my shame and guilt prevented me from looking anyone in the face.

After being rushed into surgery, I was devastated to learn that I had been five months pregnant and in labor with a baby boy. My husband was not on the premises. I vaguely remembered that I told him to leave. There was no question that the divorce would go forward.

For months, I had nightmares about where my baby was. *Did they just throw him into the dumpster like garbage?* No one had discussed any final arrangements with me, and I wasn't going to ask my husband. When I got the courage to ask for information, I learned that hospitals cremate unclaimed remains.

The word *unclaimed* almost split my heart in two. It condemned me. I could describe my life in one word: "unwanted." And now my baby boy was unwanted *and* unclaimed. I was worse than my mother. Struck with guilt and remorse, I hated myself.

The psychiatrist gave me tranquilizers to lessen my intense emotional distress. At night, I mixed the pills with alcohol to sleep and to forget for a while. To this day, I don't know how I functioned enough to go back to work. After only a few days on the job, I began cramping and fell to my knees in searing pain.

An ambulance carried me to the same emergency room. When the gynecologist on call heard the type of procedure I had undergone, she suspected the back-alley abortionist had perforated my uterus.

Fortunately, I was only suffering from an infection, and after two rounds of antibiotics and another minor surgery, the gynecologist pronounced me cured. Just as she was leaving the examination room, she turned and said, "In cases like these, you should know there is only a 1 percent chance you'll ever get pregnant again." And she was gone.

I was stunned. I stopped breathing for a minute. The doctor's disclosure only added to my *resignation*. This is what I deserved. I wasn't worthy of having a child.

Could anything be worse than the failure of a marriage and the abortion of a child? Maybe not worse, but something did happen during these same months that was almost too painful to endure.

My T—the woman I loved so dearly, my dear friend and advocate, and my aunt—committed suicide.

Around midnight one starless night, in the same bedroom where she held and comforted me as an infant, my T sat alone on her bed. Her comfort was a bottle of Wild Turkey whiskey and her father's .38 Smith and Wesson revolver.

I think I understand why she laid his gun on a piece of ordinary lined notebook paper and outlined its shape with a plain yellow school pencil. Inside the outline, she wrote the words: *I hope you're satisfied*. It was a message. What did it mean? Who was she blaming? What happened that made her write those words?

Without leaving any other message, she put the loaded pistol in her mouth and pulled the trigger.

My grandfather was sleeping in the very next room. He certainly heard the shot that killed his youngest daughter. He and my grandmother must have rushed into her room. They must have seen the piece of paper, now splattered with her blood.

It would be years later, after my grandmother's death, before anyone saw that note. It was found tucked in the back of an old dresser drawer her room.

From that night of her death, my grandparents forbade the mention of her name. The family reported to the public that she had an accident cleaning her gun. This secret, along with many others, was kept by everyone concerned. Each of us suffered in silence, honoring my grandparents' orders.

All my aunts and uncles have been dead for many years, the family secrets buried with them. I believe each of them knew the meaning of the suicide note, but no one is left to tell the whole story. If the truth sets us free, lies entrap us.

I am still grieving for my cherished young aunt. She was one of the brightest stars in my life. I have never loved anyone more or counted on anyone as much. Tears stream down my face as I write about her death. For the rest of my life, I will regret that I didn't know she needed me on that lonely night.

11
Hannah

Your people will be my people,
and your God will be my God.
Ruth 1:16

"When one door closes, another one opens" is a common optimistic saying, but in my life, doors seemed to only slam shut. The doors to my marriage, to my pregnancy, and to the life of my favorite aunt would stay closed forever. I wasn't hopeful or prepared for another door to open anytime soon.

A few months after returning to work, I parked as usual in the office garage and stepped into the crowded elevator. The same old show tunes I'd heard a hundred times were playing in the background. The elevator car stopped to let some folks off, and just as the door was closing, a handsome stranger with curly black hair sprinted toward the open door, tripped, and almost fell into my lap.

Everyone in the elevator laughed, but he blurted out a zealous apology, speaking only to me. "I'm so sorry. I almost knocked you over." He had barely bumped into me. "Are you okay?" Without taking a breath, he forged ahead with an invitation. "You'll have to let me make it up to you over lunch." He seemed completely unaware that other people were on the elevator.

Without a word, I got a business card out of my bag, handed it to him with a slight smile, and stepped out of the elevator at the next level, never expecting to hear from him again.

Within the hour, my intercom buzzed. It was the man on the elevator. "I wasn't joking about lunch," he said. "How about today? How about the Ritz?"

The Ritz? He casually threw out the name of the most luxurious hotel nearby. I'd never been in the Ritz-Carlton and wondered if I was adequately dressed. *Well, it's only lunch*, I thought. *Why not?* I agreed to meet him at the restaurant at noon.

If the elevator encounter hadn't happened in a flash, I might have noticed his well-tailored suit, his gold monogrammed cufflinks, and the Italian silk tie gracing the front of his starched white dress shirt. His appearance virtually shouted *successful* in flashing neon lights. In fact, he was successful, a *Million-Dollar Salesman,* and lunch at the Ritz was no big deal to him.

I walked through the opulent lobby and entered the restaurant. It was evident that the excessively proper maître d' knew my lunch date's name. He immediately escorted me to his table. This man I had known for all of two minutes greeted me with a long-stemmed rose and a deep bow. Many women might have been flattered by his gallant gesture, but this wasn't my first rodeo. In a matter of seconds, I was put off and on guard and wished I was somewhere else.

This man didn't know me, and I seriously doubted he would want to know me once he knew my history. I couldn't figure out if he was naive, a player, or desperate.

It never occurred to me that he was just a nice guy. With these thoughts swirling in my head, I was flustered. But I was an expert at appearing composed and charming. I smiled, engaged in small talk, and ordered the lobster bisque as the first course.

He was cheerful and friendly and seemed to genuinely enjoy my company, but I wasn't accepting that at face value. I may have looked as calm as a swan gliding over the smooth water of a lovely lake, but beneath the surface, suspicion churned the water. I was still reeling from my ex-husband's pronouncement, "No man will ever want you once they know you." I thought it was true.

Sternly reprimanding myself, I said to myself, *Get a grip, girl. Don't make such a big deal out of a casual lunch and a flower. It's not a marriage proposal. Anyway, once he knows what you just did, he will never look at you again. This is a one-time deal. You might as well enjoy your lunch.*

Enjoy, I did—following the creamy lobster bisque and crusty French bread, the entrée of tiny crisp lamb chops arrived, followed by fresh strawberries over cheesecake to complete the meal. After throwing a wad of money on the table and pulling back my chair, he escorted me down the street to the front of my office building. After a warm hug, he walked away.

Back at my desk, I was staring at that single rose and trying to get my jumbled thoughts together when he called. I hadn't been in my office for more than fifteen minutes.

"Thanks for having lunch with me. I really enjoyed meeting you. I wondered if you'd like to join me for a little cruise down the river tomorrow night."

A cruise? Really? He was moving fast. I ran the invitation through my mind: *Alone on his boat out on the* river—*a perfect set-up for seduction. Did he take me for an idiot? Did he think one expensive lunch obligated me for more?* My suspicions tripled.

So why did I accept his invitation? Partly because I liked a challenge and partly because I was curious to see what would happen. Besides, I told myself, *I can handle whatever move he makes. I can take care of myself. Why not enjoy an evening cruise?* Before I knew it, I was stepping onto his gleaming yacht.

The night couldn't have been more perfect. A cool breeze and the quiet of the river welcomed us. The setting sun threw lovely colors over the water as a backdrop. He settled me into a comfortable chair on the back deck, with a glass of fine wine. He went up to the controls, steered the boat to a secluded cove, and dropped anchor.

Here we go, I thought.

As the boat gently rocked on the water, he donned an apron with the words *I Cook for Kisses,* lit some votive candles scattered around, and poured me a second glass of wine. I was surprised when he didn't join me, and I warned myself not to drink too much. He disappeared down the narrow stairs.

In my experience, this kind of treatment required *quid pro quo.* I conjured up a rather amusing scene of my date coming up the stairs, wearing nothing but the apron. I was rehearsing my response to whatever happened when the boat captain arrived topside, fully dressed, to serve our dinner by candlelight. Years later, after he became my husband, I shared my wild fantasy. He thought my story was hilarious.

The night unveiled itself like a chaste 1950s Doris Day movie. Refusing any help to clear the dishes, he returned with a small demitasse cup of after-dinner coffee and serenaded me with his guitar. I could barely enjoy myself, wondering what would come next. Around 9:00 p.m., he put his guitar away, started the boat, and headed back to the marina, never making the move I expected.

Taking my arm, he helped me disembark from the boat and walked me to the car. He thanked me for a lovely evening, gave me a bear hug, and kissed me gently on the lips. With a big wave, he watched as I drove away from the marina.

I was bewildered, wondering if he was gay or if I had done or said something wrong. I'd never been with a man who didn't want something sexual. What did he want?

He called every day and night that week, and although we had long conversations on the phone, I told him almost nothing about my past except that I was divorced. On Friday, he suggested we return to the Ritz for lunch. After we sat down, he casually pulled a ring box out of his pocket and placed it on the table in front of me. The past week had been so surreal, I wouldn't have been surprised if he had dropped to one knee and proposed right then and there. I was speechless.

He extended the box toward me and popped it open to reveal a large topaz stone encircled in gold. Topaz is my birthstone, but my birthday was over a month away. It was much too much and much too soon.

Instead of showing appreciation for the gift, I sat silently staring at the box. I was annoyed and agitated, but I tried to slow my breathing and think clearly: *What's wrong with you? Accept the gift. Thank him. This is what nice men do for the women they like.*

But I couldn't play the part of a normal girl any longer. This man had no idea who I was. His generosity and attention would vanish in a split second when he knew more about me, so I didn't want his gift meant for the girl he thought I was. I couldn't let this charade go on. I would end the relationship before he dumped me.

I'm sure my silence surprised him. But what I said surprised him even more. "I'm sure this is how you treat all the women you date. Your overly extravagant gestures make me think you don't believe you have much to offer but your money."

He looked at me in stunned silence, still holding the ring box in his hand. He stood slowly and tossed the box on the table with some money. Looking at me as directly as I had looked at him, he shook his head and said, "You've got some serious problems." And with that statement, he walked out of the Ritz and out of my life.

I didn't hear a word from him. He was right about me having problems. I fretted and stewed over what now seemed like very foolish behavior. Whatever had caused my outburst, my words had clearly ended the relationship.

A few weeks later, my phone rang just before noon. The voice I didn't think I would hear again asked, "Would a McDonald's be more to your liking?"

I didn't know whether to laugh or cry.

We met in a small park across the street from my office. He sat there with a big smile and two McDonald's bags.

"I didn't want to go overboard on the order." He handed me the small hamburger sack without the usual drink or fries.

He dove right in and told me why he'd called. "Your words caused me to wonder how other people see me, so I asked a few friends. They agreed with you that I can be quite a showoff. They conceded that others might see me as arrogant and conceited, and they don't understand why I do it, when I'm a really likable guy."

He tearfully confessed that maybe he did feel inferior about some things. His vulnerability touched my heart, and I was able to admit that it was some of my own insecurities that made it difficult for me to accept his generosity. I touched his face to dab some mustard off his chin, and he took my hand and kissed it. My defenses melted a bit.

A friendship began that afternoon in the park. He turned the volume down on his showmanship, and I found him to be the same down-to-earth likable guy his friends knew. I began to feel safe.

We went to the movies, walked my dog, and occasionally had an outlandishly expensive meal. As we grew close, this successful businessman explained why he felt inferior. Unlike the Jewish boys in his childhood circle of friends, he hadn't attained the name doctor or lawyer as most of them had. He had only finished high school, and no matter how much money he made, he would always be just a salesman in his own eyes.

I applauded what he'd accomplished. "You didn't need a formal education. You're a self-made man, a Renaissance man. You do everything with your whole heart, and you do it well. People admire you. They like you." He basked in my sincere compliments.

I genuinely cared for him, and although I was not passionately attracted to him, I thought that was a good thing. Passion had created unwanted drama in my life. I felt relaxed and safe in our quiet, congenial friendship and romance. He thrived on my applause and acceptance, and I felt secure because he needed me. *If he needs me, he won't get rid of me.*

His warm extended family was an added bonus to our relationship. Aunts, uncles, cousins, and even his Russian grandmother embraced me as his girlfriend. The acceptance was a tonic to my ailing self-image. Our whirlwind romance made it easy for him not to peer too deeply into my family history.

When he did get down on one knee and open a ring box, a beautiful solitary diamond sparkled in the sunlight.

I happily said, "Yes, I will marry you."

We met with the Rabbi of the reform synagogue, who had known my fiancé for many years. The Rabbi grinned at me and said he had never seen a man so happy. We discussed the process of my conversion and our subsequent marriage. Our plans were moving along very quickly.

The Rabbi said I would be immersed in the temple pool as part of the conversion ritual and marriage preparation. I saw it as a baptism I'd never had. The immersion would cleanse the past. I was hopeful that a Jewish G-d would welcome me and help me become the person I wanted to be. My intentions were heartfelt and deeply sincere. After my conversion, I was given the Hebrew name Hannah, meaning "full of grace," and we received permission to be married under the traditional wedding canopy.

We planned a small wedding with his family. I bought a lovely off-white dress, and flowers were woven into my long hair. My parents did not participate, and I was glad they were not there on my wedding day. I forget what excuse I gave for their absence. When my new husband ritually smashed a glass with his heel at the end of the ceremony, his relatives sent us off with hugs and kisses and farewell cries of *mazel tov.*

We drove away as husband and wife to begin our lives together. When I entered the honeymoon suite, I was embraced by the fragrance of dozens of roses. I suddenly thought, *I like being spoiled. My husband's kindness and attention may mend me after all.*

I was grateful to him and wanted very much to fulfill the duties of a good Jewish wife. I shopped at the kosher market, prepared traditional meals, and set a lovely dinner table in our formal dining room using our wedding crystal and china. I enjoyed an entire bottle of wine as I cooked dinner, and it never occurred to me that my indulgence was out of the ordinary. I never felt tipsy, just happy.

After six contented months, we began construction on my dream home in the country. My husband's grand gestures no longer annoyed or troubled me. I welcomed them. We hired a well-known interior designer, and during the year our home was being built, the decorator helped me find treasures to adorn every nook and cranny of our house.

To celebrate our move, we hosted a catered dinner in our "great room." White tablecloths shone dramatically against the dark wood floor. Bouquets of fresh wildflowers, native to our area, graced every table. Waiters served drinks from silver trays.

After a delicious meal, the men retired to the back deck that spanned the entire length of the house, where they enjoyed their cigars and after-dinner drinks. I gave the ladies a grand tour of the place before we joined the gentlemen. Gradually, the conversations grew quiet, and the country sounds of crickets and tree frogs serenaded us. Stars and lightning bugs twinkled in the dark. I loved my life.

I enjoyed the quiet of the day as much as the lavish parties. When I had no errands to run, I planted flowers in large urns on the porch or cut the grass on the big riding mower. After a shower to cool off, I lay nude on the deck, with a little gin in my fresh lemonade. Bob Dylan, James Brown, and Marvin Gaye played in the background. Sometimes I got a little wild, dancing to the beat of the music. I wanted to keep the past in the past, but a part of me missed those wild boozy days.

Every evening, I primped for my husband's arrival from the office and greeted him with a big smile and open arms. I continued cooking dinner, but gradually we ate less often in the dining room and more frequently ate on a tray in front of the television. News commentators and actors provided most of the dialog during our meal.

I felt lonely and unfairly ignored when the news seemed more interesting than me. I wanted my husband's attention back like in the early days of our marriage when he only had eyes for me. I began to wilt like a flower without water and didn't realize that my resentment was about a great deal more than met the eye.

My husband was a good man, satisfied with simple things. A good meal, a good cigar, a couple of hours of TV, occasional sex, and a good night's sleep was all he needed to be a contented man.

I tried to count my blessings. I tried to be rational. At some level, I knew the intensity of my feelings made no sense. No one was harming me. Everything in my life had changed for the better. Why couldn't I be satisfied? I felt as if some demon creature high-jacked my brain and my self-control. I didn't know the demon's name. I only knew it made me cry and complain.

My husband was attentive and concerned. He wanted to help. "Just tell me what to do."

But I was inconsolable.

What could he do? What could anyone do? I couldn't tell him how to help, because I didn't understand what was happening.

He tried to find the reason for my unhappiness. "Are you feeling lonely out here in the country? Do you want to move back to the city? Do you need a vacation?" Finally, he said, "Honey, what about a baby? Everyone's asking when we expect the pitter-patter of little feet." He tried to say it jokingly, but I knew he wanted children.

I knew this day would come. What if the doctor's prediction of sterility was correct? I wished I had done the fair thing and told my husband before we married that I might be barren.

I should have told him. Now, I had to live with the dread that my abortion would somehow be revealed if I didn't conceive. He would be horrified, and what would he do with me then?

He painted a pretty portrait of us as parents. He described the fun we would have on vacations, holidays, and at family gatherings. He promised I would have all the help I needed with the house and the baby. I began to entertain the idea of motherhood. Maybe I wasn't sterile.

I imagined what our child would look like. I hoped it would be a boy with curly black hair like his daddy. Maybe that little boy *was* what I needed. Every time I imagined the boy, he was laughing.

I thought of the benefits. *Would holding a child against my body finally fill the emptiness from my mother's rejection? Would it somehow absolve me from the sin of abortion? Would bringing a life into the world make up for the life I took?*

74

Maybe I could do it. Hoping to become pregnant, I stopped taking the pill and quit drinking alcohol. I welcomed the idea more and more. I looked at baby clothes and cribs, almost forgetting the possibility that it might not happen.

When I didn't get pregnant after four months, my husband's sperm count was tested. There was no medical reason he couldn't produce a child, so it was my turn to visit the doctor. I dreaded what he would find, but he couldn't tell that I had had an abortion. He encouraged us to keep trying and said it was not unusual for a first pregnancy to take a little time.

Four more slow months passed with no child in my womb. I felt sick, but not from morning sickness. I began to have such vivid memories of the abortion that it nauseated me. I knew I was being punished and that I would never get pregnant. And now, my innocent husband was being punished for what I had done.

I lived in fear and shame. My resolve not to drink alcohol seemed irrelevant, because I wasn't pregnant. In fact, I reasoned that a little alcohol would calm me and chase the ghosts of my past away. I spent my afternoons drinking on the deck, listening to Peggy Lee sing "Is That All There Is?"

Peggy was singing my song. The lyrics told of a woman's life that was missing something. She even asked herself in the song, "Why go on? Why shouldn't I just end it all?" Like me, she didn't know what was missing. Her solution was the same as mine—break out the booze and keep dancing. I no longer felt like dancing, but I did want the alcohol.

Soon, the fact that I had been drinking long before the glass of wine I had with dinner became obvious. My husband looked at me across the table with tears in his eyes. We postponed any chance of getting pregnant. I lost my appetite and stopped cooking or cleaning. I moved into the guest bedroom, because I woke up at all hours of the night weeping. He thought my angst was because we had stopped trying to get pregnant, but he only saw a tiny tip of the iceberg. He had no idea how much trauma was hidden below the waterline.

He did everything in his power to love me, but no amount of love, money, or attention from another human being could fix me. I didn't know if there was anything that would save me.

As surely as the blessing of hope in the temple pool had lifted me, depression's curse was crushing me. That hope was gone. I admitted to my husband that this wasn't my first bout with severe depression, and I needed professional help.

12

Good Medicine

Weep for her. Give her medicine.
Perhaps she can yet be healed.
Jeremiah 51:8

Even as we looked for a doctor, I was skeptical. Was there
really any medicine that would keep me from getting
depressed over and over? I had been over-medicated and
under-helped by psychiatry too many times to be
optimistic.

When we were referred to a local seminary rather than
a doctor, I was even more skeptical. I almost refused to
go, but this Ph.D. counselor gave us promising
information, and I was willing to hear more.

In his opinion, all human behavior made sense. If I
could hear the internal conversations in my mind, I could
better understand my behavior. His theory was that many
of my feelings and reactions stemmed from childhood. He
didn't deny that I needed medication but said, "Medicine
doesn't heal. It stabilizes mood and controls symptoms."
Therapy would help me understand the "why" motivating
my behavior to make better decisions and talk to myself
differently.

He practiced *Transactional Analysis*, a therapy that focused on relationships and childhood development and how it affects our adult lives.

He provided a list of symptoms common in people who had been abused as children:

- Low self-esteem
- Poor boundaries with others
- Self-hatred
- Shame
- Anxiety
- Hopelessness
- Anger
- Impulsiveness
- Magical thinking
- Rebellion
- Despair
- Depression
- Self-destructive behavior
- Self-medication with substance and process addictions

I had every symptom. After carefully listening to the story of my childhood and about the decisions I had made, the counselor explained my diagnosis in layman's terms: "You've been wounded by trauma and abuse that began early in your life. You were shamed and told lies about yourself that you believe. You are living in reaction to the past and don't realize what is causing your feelings. You criticize and blame yourself without compassion and then try to be perfect. Perfectionism is the worst form of self-abuse. You will only be able to create and maintain a healthy lifestyle if you can forgive and love yourself."

What gave me the most hope was that the therapist didn't see me as a problem to be fixed but as a person who needed help and deserved compassion rather than blame. He said I could change my life.

Did I dare hope to believe him? Questions swirled in my head as I tried to comprehend. Did my feelings make sense? Could I make better choices? Could I live in the present despite everything I had done? Could I forgive myself?

He didn't sugarcoat the fact that I had a chemical imbalance and a clinical diagnosis that required medication to stabilize my thinking and feelings. Although he didn't think alcohol and drug use was the core issue, he adamantly said I must stay clean and sober to succeed.

Before he would agree to treat me, I had to agree that I would not engage in any kind of dangerous behavior whatsoever. "If you are willing to do what I ask," he said, "I am willing to help you face the painful reality of what happened to you, allow you to experience your feelings constructively, straighten out your thinking, and embrace yourself with love and care. You can create the life you want."

I gladly agreed to everything. In my own handwriting, I made the commitment to live. We began marital therapy as a couple, and I joined one of his weekly therapy groups for women. My mood and our marriage improved rapidly as I began to understand the theory behind his treatment.

During weekly group therapy, women regularly commented that my insights into what they were feeling were so accurate, it was like I was in their skin. They felt understood and encouraged by my feedback. The therapist told my husband and me that I had the natural ability and inclinations to be a good therapist. If my experiences could help others, I could find value in even the worst parts of my life.

As my husband educated himself about mental illness and the aftermath of childhood trauma, he forgave my less-than-stellar performance as his wife. He and I investigated the educational requirements to become a psychologist. When we found a master's program in psychology at a local university, he blessed me with a full financial ride to attain the degree.

I threw all my energy into graduate school, initially driving into town three nights a week. Since my classes ended so late in the evening, we agreed that I would stay with a school friend two nights a week. We re-homed our dog, because we couldn't spend enough time with him—something I never thought I could do.

I was more than grateful for the opportunity my husband gave me to become a psychologist. From my perspective, life was ideal. Even though we were spending less time together, we still caught a movie, attended game nights with his relatives, made love, and slept in on weekends. He had given up his boat, because we lived in the country, but we enjoyed projects around the house and yard.

For me, things were easy and pleasant, and my husband seemed content. It was only later that I saw he was too fearful of upsetting me to mention his unhappiness. He made no demands, even in our joint marital therapy sessions. With no complaints from him, I saw no need to continue marriage counseling, and we stopped going to appointments together.

I was way too busy to see beyond my own goals, and our therapist failed us as a couple. He should have confronted me about putting my husband so far down on my priority list and should have encouraged my husband to express his feelings.

While my focus was on learning how to help every hurting person I met, I didn't see how much the person next to me was hurting. I grasped so intensely at that golden ring of self-worth I'd never had, I became self-focused, self-centered, and insensitive to his needs. My husband deserved much more than gratitude.

I graduated in record time with high honors and high hopes. When I began an internship at the state mental hospital, I was in heaven, a strange term for the hell-hole of a government-run hospital. My life was worth something, because I was going to help others. My self-esteem soared.

Interns were assigned to the *back ward* patients who had been in the hospital the longest and were not expected to leave. I had always believed if someone had loved me enough to rescue me, my whole life would have been different. If I could give these most-discouraged patients enough kindness, care, and attention, I might salvage some of them. Maybe I could bring them out of the stupor created by antipsychotic medication and hopelessness.

Some did make small positive changes, if only to smile for the first time in a long time. With each tiny victory I observed, I cried for joy. As the semester wore on, those exciting moments of success were overshadowed by my perception of unfairness in the state mental health system.

I was angry with the attending physicians, who seemed cold and disinterested, mostly sedating the patients. I was mad at the families who never visited and with the state because the hospital was understaffed. These patients hadn't caused their illness. No one was trying to understand what happened to them in childhood or what they needed now. The hospital met basic physical needs, but there was no therapy.

More could have been done to help the patients, but my resentment and desperate need to help them wasn't just about the system. The hospital conditions triggered my own childhood feelings—the feelings I had as a lonely little girl wishing someone would rescue me.

I didn't tell anyone, not my husband nor my therapist, that I was becoming overwhelmed by this seemingly hopeless situation. I bit my lip constantly to keep from expressing my anger or bursting into tears. I was afraid I would get jerked out of the internship if anyone knew how distraught I felt. I didn't want to lose my hopes and dreams of becoming a psychologist.

By the time the internship was over, I couldn't keep up the charade. During the summer break, I confessed everything to my therapist, and he admitted me to the hospital. After a week of rest, new medication, and recalibrating my thinking, I stabilized once more.

But my husband realized he had gotten in over his head. My ups and downs were too much for him to handle. I understood how he felt. I had to live with me too. I encouraged him to get a divorce. He reluctantly agreed it was best for him, and he was beyond generous, supporting me until I graduated and hung up my shingle to practice. He was always a *mensch*—a really stand-up guy. I wish I could have been the person I wanted to be for him.

I looked forward to every appointment in my new office. I was dedicated to helping patients thrive. Facing challenging life situations had created a profound understanding and caring empathy for suffering people. A wise clinical supervisor cautioned me about realistic expectations and defined the boundaries of responsibility for therapists. Months rolled into years, and patients walked out of my office with hope and plans for a better future. I was continually surprised by the human spirit's resilience, and I was delighted to be part of each person's healing journey.

How did things go wrong? Because helping other people fight their "demons" is not the same as dealing with your own guilt, depression, and foreboding. I envied my patients when they left the office to return to their lives and relationships. I was intimately connected on an emotional level, but I was not friends with my patients. When I turned off the office lights, I often wished I had me as a friend to go home to.

By day, I was a successful, busy woman. Counseling others distracted and gratified me. But in the quiet of the night, insomnia, restlessness, and loneliness clutched me. No matter how I tried to focus on my victories and how many wet kisses I got from my new puppy, I felt empty and alone. I spent a fortune on massages and activities, hoping touch and companionship with others would help me feel less lonely. It was a temporary fix for a real relationship. It is hard to look back at these facts. It should have been so evident that my lack of trust in others and my dislike of myself created my loneliness.

When the emptiness got the best of me, when I couldn't shake off those lonesome feelings, I foolishly thought a little alcohol would ease my pain. Rather than help, alcohol eased me into the night to pursue connection with anyone I could find. The bar clothing came on— short skirt, high heels, and black-seamed stockings. The die was cast, and I didn't turn back.

It wasn't sex I was looking for, but if sex was a way to be held and cuddled, I was more than willing. I didn't even want to have sex with most of the men I met, but these strangers filled a need, at least temporarily. The relief walked out the door with the man. I vowed I would never repeat my behavior, but like any addict, I would search for my fix again.

Finally, I thought I had found the perfect solution. I met a straight male who agreed to be a "friend without benefits." For weeks, we slept together without having sex, and I got the comfort I craved. I was content, but he started pushing to have sex.

When I confronted him about our agreement, he said the same thing my husband had said years before. "Are you kidding? I just thought you wanted to take it slow. No grown man is going to be your teddy bear. What's your problem? What are you, a child?"

He didn't know how right he was. I was looking for the comfort of motherly love from a man. How crazy is that? I didn't even respond to his words. A part of me gave up and gave in. We had sex, and I never saw him again. *Good riddance*, I thought.

Never dreaming I could get pregnant, I hadn't used birth control. A few months later, when a pregnancy stick revealed the plus sign, I couldn't believe my eyes. I wasn't barren—another fetus lived in my womb.

My second abortion was easy to obtain and clinically sterile. In less than three hours, the medical staff ended a life and had me back in my car. Part of me felt destroyed in the process. I pressed my hands against my chest to comfort my broken heart. I wanted to wail or scream, but I could barely breathe.

On that sunny day when everything around me seemed so dark, I made a vow. Never! Never again would this happen. No more lives would be snuffed out due to my poor choices. I must find a permanent solution.

I consulted a gynecologist regarding sterilization. With a history of depression and self-destructive actions coupled with two abortions, he agreed to my request. Even though I was only in my late twenties, the surgery was performed. I felt numb and hollow after the procedure, but I tried to assure myself that I had done the right thing.

13

Mothering

God places the lonely in families.
Psalm 68:6

My attempts at reassurance were defeated by agonizing
guilt and sorrow. Every step I took felt like pulling myself
through deep water. I wanted to crumble in a heap and
never get up, but I did my best to keep going and act like
nothing was wrong. I couldn't escape my actions. My
thoughts returned to the offense time-after-time. I needed
help, but I certainly couldn't go to a grief group. Grief was
reserved for those who had lost someone they loved. I
hadn't lost someone. I had destroyed someone, and I
didn't deserve the privilege of grieving.

I finally went back to my old therapy group, and those
dear women helped me recognize that I was the one
punishing myself. I thought others would do the same, but
they didn't show disgust or contempt—only care and good
will. They recounted the many times I had lifted them up
with empathy and compassion. They reminded me that, as
humans, we all fall short and make mistakes. But I felt that
what I had done was unforgiveable. I would need a true

change of heart to overcome the negative feelings I had about myself.

Their words began to penetrate the darkness of my self-contempt. I had little chance of moving forward unless I had compassion for myself. I had been trying to understand myself for years, but forgiveness requires more than understanding. It would require loving and accepting myself, despite what I had done.

I managed to feel a little sympathy for what I went through as a child, but that was no excuse for the wrongs I'd committed. Maybe sympathy was a place I could start. I recalled one time when I stumbled across a picture of myself as a little girl. I had such a strong reaction, I wanted to reach into the picture and hold her close. I looked into her pretty, innocent face and wondered how anyone could mistreat her.

Once I started thinking about that little girl, I couldn't stop thinking about her. I imagined her standing in front of me. She seemed to be waiting for me to do something. But you can't go back and rescue your child years later. Or could you?

Suddenly I wanted to see every photograph ever taken of her. I searched my mother's house and found an old tattered box spilling over with the black-and-white photos that were sent to my father overseas. I was touched that somehow he kept those pictures all through the war and brought them home. The box also contained a baby book with pages yellowed with age.

The baby book was entirely void of entries other than my name, date, time of birth, and the usual newborn hospital photo. I felt a pang of sadness that my mother never wrote anything in the book, never recording any highlights of my life. I studied the features of this tiny

87

infant and felt a rush of wonder and tenderness. She didn't look too happy about being born. I found myself smiling, talking to her as if she were really there.

Was I losing my mind, developing a split personality, becoming psychotic? Was this a bizarre attempt to find an innocent part of me that hadn't made all those terrible mistakes and was worthy of love? Where would this end?

I didn't know the answer to any of those questions. I only knew I wanted to love her. I wanted to write something in that empty baby book. Frankly, I didn't care what my behavior might mean. I embraced the task of honoring and cherishing the child in those photos as best I could. I think I felt as enthusiastic and excited as an expectant mother who *wants* her child.

I lovingly pasted my childhood photos into the book and wrote messages from my heart all around them— messages I'd never heard from my mother:

I'm glad you were born.
You are the child I have always wanted.
You are a beautiful girl.
Your needs are natural.
It is my joy and privilege to take care of you.

The words I wrote in the book disputed the lies spoken to me. I recorded a cassette tape of positive messages and listened to my affirming words as I drifted off to sleep. To the very best of my ability, I adopted myself.

The fantasy became a kind of reality. I had a child to raise. I needed to take care of her properly. I questioned myself. *Would I pour alcohol down my child's throat? Would I put three Twinkies into my child's stomach? Would I expose my child to a man I didn't know?*

The answer was always no, no, and no! I listened to my own nurturing voice. I stopped smoking and drinking. I started dieting and practicing yoga. As weeks and months passed, I improved physically and emotionally. I wondered, *If I had known I could parent, would I have been able to mother a child?* I would never know the answer to that haunting question.

I legally changed my surname to a name that reflected my newfound value. I didn't want any man's name—not an ex-husband's name or my father's name. I was creating my own family, even though it was a family of one.

The more I saw myself as worthy, the more I wanted to help others know their value. I especially wanted to help those who had been beaten down as children and stop abuse before it happened. I believed I had suffered much more than necessary because no one intervened on my behalf. With growing confidence, I became even more determined to fulfill my vow to defend the helpless.

No matter when or where it happened, if I saw a child or animal being slapped or jerked around, I went a little out of my mind. I yelled, "Stop it!" in parking lots, grocery stores, and dressing rooms. Yelling drew a lot of attention to the situation. After my initial reaction, I tried to calm myself and rationally talk to the person. I would hand them my "doctor" business card with the promise: "If you ever need help, contact me for free." Not one person ever accepted my offer.

I considered my actions to be admirable. I was a neighborhood watch of one—an avenging angel, a vigilante defending the defenseless and righting wrongs. In actuality, I was having flashbacks to the violence I had experienced as a child. I couldn't protect myself then, but I could do something now.

While walking my dog in the park one day, I heard a dog's frantic cries. Obviously, the dog was in great distress. I picked up my dog and ran in the direction of the cries. I saw a man whipping his small dog. I rushed at him, screaming. I believe I would have attacked him physically if he hadn't stopped. He cursed me, shook his fist at me, and thankfully, walked away.

In today's climate of gun violence, I might not be alive telling this story. In my efforts to help others, I was putting "my own child" in harm's way. Any one of those perpetrators could have turned on me. My vigilante tactics could not continue without someone getting hurt. I needed to bridle my anger into a disciplined approach that would help victims in the safest way possible.

But what was the best way to help? I could become a court advocate, volunteer in a women's shelter, or work for organizations that helped sexually and physically abused women.

But I didn't need to go outside my practice. Abused people came into my office every day. The issue was not *who* to help or *where* to help, but *how* to help. Talk therapy didn't seem adequate for what so many abused clients needed.

Looking for answers, I read about an institute established to *re-parent* people with debilitating mental illnesses caused by childhood trauma. The patients came to live in a homelike setting for at least a year, where doctors and therapists became their surrogate moms and dads. This is what I had been trying to do on my own. My idea wasn't so crazy or unrealistic.

The doctors encouraged their patients to regress to the age of their trauma, no matter when it occurred, even during birth or infancy. They provided a way for the patient to re-experience the trauma in safety with age-appropriate discipline and guidance. They theorized that a "corrective emotional experience" could reprogram the brain.

If they had been abused or abandoned as infants, they were held and bottle-fed. They heard many of the same messages I had been speaking to myself. If they needed to have a kicking, screaming "terrible two" tantrum, they were allowed to do so safely, without harming themselves or others. If they needed to cry, they were comforted. Whatever the situation, they were offered a compassionate, corrective experience.

Most of the "hopelessly ill" patients improved rapidly in the structured, nurturing environment. The changes were remarkable. Hallucinations stopped, and they regulated their former "crazy" behavior. They responded well to parental requests, and their previously disheveled, unkempt appearance changed. They not only felt better physically and emotionally, but they also looked better.

Eventually, these patients could rationally discuss what happened to them. They could describe the irrational and false internal dialog that fueled their "acting-out" behavior. Staff "moms" and "dads" saw their wards reverse the early hopelessness and frustration and began to make plans that could create an independent future. These changes occurred without medication.

The practice was controversial, but I believed this type of intervention could be used to some extent in an out-patient treatment setting. Almost simultaneously, two young women came to my office in dire need of help. One was withdrawn and fearful, the other so violent that she had recently been arrested. They needed more than traditional once-a-week talk therapy, but a psychiatric hospital would only medicate and release them. Re-parenting could be immensely beneficial to them, helping them in record time, but neither could afford to go to the Institute. Was there a way I could re-parent them on my own?

A re-parenting training was scheduled for my area of the country. Therapists brought their own patients and were assisted in helping them resolve early traumas. I would stand in as the "surrogate parent" during the process. I explained the theory to the two women, and they were willing to participate.

As a result of rewarding experiences in the workshop, we three agreed I would act as their surrogate mother. I had so often said, "If only someone had stepped in. If only someone had protected me. If only someone had cared enough." I wanted to save them from the years of suffering and poor choices I had made. I embraced the challenge.

Those years were demanding for the girls and for me. At times, I failed to provide the structure they needed, but they knew they were loved and wanted. Parenting my girls has been the most incredible experience of my life. I didn't give birth to them, but they were my daughters.

I have watched the transformation of my lovely "older daughter" for decades now. She makes a profound difference in the lives or many people as a therapist. I have no adequate words to describe the blessing of holding her two precious infants in my arms. Having granddaughters is indeed a miracle when you've never had a child.

Although my younger daughter never wholly recovered from the abuse she endured and continued to medicate her pain with drugs and alcohol, she knew she was loved before succumbing to cancer a few years later.

Adults abused as children can heal, but the more significant issue is how to prevent the harm from ever occurring. Since most childhood abuse occurs at the hands of caretakers, it seemed obvious that intervention and help was needed for them.

Today, one can go online and take classes to prepare for childbirth and baby care and learn about infant safety. Men can attend a daddy boot camp. No such opportunities were available in the 1970s.

Deeply personal emotional issues drove my desire to impact early childhood parenting in a positive way: my mother's undiagnosed post-partum depression, fear that I couldn't be a good mother to my own children, two abortions, sterilization, and my early childhood vow to save any living creature from harm. I wanted to turn what had happened to my mother and me into something good.

In the 1960s, most women unrealistically expected themselves to keep a spotless house, look as beautiful as a movie star, and always be insanely happy over being a mother. Women were often heard apologizing for tears or frustration after childbirth, saying, "I just don't know what's wrong with me. I should be happy." They weren't happy, and they were ashamed and tried to look happy.

If I could find ways for a community to provide help to families, then the mothers, fathers, and children would all benefit. What was more important than loving and respecting children? But many people didn't have important information on how to take care of themselves, which is necessary for healthy parenting. All kinds of ideas came to mind. High school and college curriculum could offer classes on the needs of children, requirements for healthy relationships, and get counseling for their own problems. Planning programs within churches could provide better child care, supportive counseling, and parenting classes. I was keenly aware that most doctors would benefit from continuing education about men and children in trouble. More information on abuse can be found in women's public restrooms than in doctor's offices. The community needed to help parents in the early days of child care.

With all these ideas swirling in my head, I would need the proper credentials in order to fund and implement any of these programs. Medical school was too daunting, both in time and money. At the age of thirty-seven, I decided to throw all my effort into a graduate school doctoral program. I was determined to be part of the solution to this pervasive problem.

I was hyper-focused on my studies, to the exclusion of almost everything else, including making friends. But I did overhear some of the students talking about their spirituality. I surely wasn't interested in religion, but what was this spirituality? Eventually, I joined them in studying Enlightenment through Edgar Casey's teaching and became a Mastermind group member. It was fun to get Tarot card readings and seek to understand myself through numerology and astrology. I sought higher consciousness through meditation and yoga.

When I completed all the required course work in record time, I gave myself a well-deserved vacation before I dove into the rigorous discipline required to write a dissertation. My research would focus on the condition and possible provisions for pregnant women, especially in the low-income population. The pain and regret of my abortions might serve some good after all.

14

East West

*Satan, who is the god of this world, has blinded
the minds of those who don't believe.
2 Corinthians 4:4*

My friend and I took off for some sun and fun on the
West Coast. We didn't want to be totally frivolous and
hedonistic, so we decided to visit some famous meditation
centers along the way.

We landed in Los Angeles, picked up our rental car,
and headed straight for the Bodhi Tree bookstore, a
Mecca for New Age seekers. The store was literally
wrapped around an ancient Indian Bodhi tree and was the
best place to learn what was happening in the California
community.

While perusing the many flyers attached to the
enormous tree, we saw an advertisement to "lose your
mind and find your joy" in the ashram (retreat center) of
Bhagwan Shree Rajneesh. We'd never heard of this guru,
but joy was exactly what we sought. Obviously, we had
arrived right on time, because the event was happening
that night. We would be there when the doors opened.

At the rather gaudy building, we were greeted with the traditional namaste bow and led into a dimly lit room where sixty strangers sat on the floor in silence. To one side, live musicians played soft Indian music on the sitar and flute. After a short time, we were given blindfolds and were invited to become "one with the music." The doors closed. Sometimes I think these early chapters should be called Closed Doors.

Wanting to fully participate in the moment, I swayed to the notes' slow cadence. Gradually, the tempo accelerated, and I experienced an uninhibited burst of energy. Feet moving, arms flung to the sky, body twisting and turning, I forgot about everything outside that room. When the music abruptly stopped, the whole lot of us collapsed in a pile on the floor. I had just experienced my first "dynamic meditation."

I'm glad we were blindfolded, because many of the attendees had shed most, if not all, of their clothing. As we began to find our belongings, I noticed that many people were wearing bright orange garments. Not a word was spoken as we arranged ourselves on the floor, facing a small platform.

A side door opened, and a small bearded man entered the room. With his head slightly bowed, his hands in the namaste position of prayer and greeting, he nodded to the assembly and seated himself in an easy chair on the stage. Instead of fanfare announcing the arrival of Bhagwan Shree Rajneesh, a veil of peacefulness settled around us.

He wore a simple white garment and sandals. He may have been small, but his command over the room was immeasurable. There wasn't a sound as he slowly spoke to us in a deliberate but kind and gentle voice. He smiled and nodded as he spoke.

His deep brown eyes and direct stare mesmerized me. I felt condemned when the preacher stared at me all those years ago, but when Rajneesh's gaze rested on me, I felt loved. When Bhagwan raised his hand, he blessed. The pastor's raised hand had felt threatening.

I have no memory of what Rajneesh said. I just remember that I wanted to climb up on that platform and lay my head in his lap. I had never felt this way about another human being except for my father.

Rajneesh was the father figure for hundreds of orange-clad idealistic people, young and old, many of whom were wealthy and highly educated. His followers, called *sannyasins*, lived with him as one family in India. If I hadn't invested so much time and money in graduate school, I would have left for India right then and there. Instead, I made plans to finish the next semester and head to India during the summer break.

Back at school, I stayed in touch with Rajneesh's teaching by listening to his talks to the Poona followers. As I heard him speak, he often mentioned Jesus. That was surprising, since he was certainly not a Christian. He considered Jesus to be one of the Enlightened Masters and quoted his words often. When he said that Jesus liked to hang out with sinners, I thought, for the first time, that he might have liked me.

The New Age point of view was appealing to many of us. The belief that in this lifetime or another we all get home to God was a great relief to me. Believing that a loving God would never send anyone to Hell made me want to shout hallelujah. Even though it might take many lifetimes for me to get my act together, I would eventually get home to God.

There was no damnation. It would all work out. No problem, nothing to worry about. This premise was a thousand times more appealing than eternity in Hell.

I didn't like the fierce Christian God of the Old Testament, who showed no mercy. Somewhere in those pages, God said he would always be with us and protect us. He hadn't protected me.

I didn't like Christians either. How dare they tell me I was going to Hell if I didn't choose to follow Jesus. Indeed, God saw their rigid, arrogant ideas as hypocrisy.

Rajneesh was right in line with the hippie philosophy. I didn't understand the Gospel, the *Good News*. What was good about it? I didn't get it, and I wasn't interested in learning. I had found another way.

15

Some Enchanted Evening

For everything there is a season, a time
for every activity . . . A time to cry . . .
A time to grieve . . . A time to search
and a time to quit searching.
Ecclesiastes 3:1-6

India remained a beacon of light through the drudgery of writing a dissertation. For the next few months, I spent hours in the library and integrated the research into my writing. I was determined to get that darn degree finished and take off to India.

When classmates invited me for an evening out at an upscale singles bar, I decided to give myself a break. I had no idea that the evening would change everything.

With the first few drinks, the place took on a lovely glow, and the unfinished dissertation that constantly hung over my head disappeared. I felt light-hearted and liberated from the grind of studying.

And then, just like in the movies, my eyes locked with a good-looking man across the crowded room. It couldn't have been more romantic unless Frank Sinatra had been singing "Some Enchanted Evening" in the background.

He beckoned me with a grin and a nod. I was drawn to him like a moth to the flame. From past experience, this intense instant attraction should have been a warning,

We spent the evening talking and dancing, exchanged phone numbers, and made a date for the following Friday at my apartment. It didn't seem to bother him one bit that my apartment was ninety miles away. It was unspoken but understood that he would stay for the weekend. The apartment was sparkling clean, and numerous long-playing records were stacked on the record player. I stocked the fridge with breakfast food and laid out fresh fruit, fine cheese, French bread, and wine for our evening repast.

When he walked through the door that night, Kenny Rogers was singing *Lady* in the background. Kenny sings that a pretty lady will change the solitary man's life. Were the words prophetic? We spent the weekend talking long into the night, snuggling and lovemaking. I felt nurtured and safe in his embrace.

Now it was my turn to visit his apartment back in the city. After class on Friday, a friend dropped me off at his apartment, and I was in his care. Located in a charming older neighborhood, the apartment was decorated with an eye for detail. After serving both of us a drink, he handed me an innocent-looking manila folder, followed by the statement: "You need to know about this."

I was about to discover he had omitted some crucial details during our first weekend together. I opened the folder and saw a newspaper clipping. The word *stabbed*, *death*, and *suicide* jumped out of the headline that read: LOCAL BUSINESSMAN STABBED. WIFE'S DEATH RULED A SUICIDE.

The article described a horrifying scene. A woman had been found dead, lying in a pool of her own blood.

Neighbors had called police after a bleeding man banged on their door and collapsed. He had been stabbed in the back. Police found another stabbing victim. A woman was lying dead in a pool of her own blood, a fatal stab wound to her heart. Strangely, she was holding the large knife in her hand.

After an investigation, police ruled the woman's death a suicide, based primarily on a note admitting to her sons her plan to kill her husband and then herself. She almost succeeded. Sitting next to me was the man who had survived this trauma, who had been stabbed in the back.

No warning bell went off. I didn't have a single thought about why this man's wife wanted to kill him or herself. I felt nothing but sympathy for the handsome, charming stranger. Obviously, he married a deranged woman, and she was entirely responsible for that terrible morning.

We put the folder away, and I put the information into the past. I'd had a lifetime of training in the art of forgetting. The past had nothing to do with our relationship. After three glorious months of courtship filled with nights of dancing, drinking, and romance, I married the man I thought was the love of my life.

Almost overnight, my romantic husband turned into a sullen stranger. I sent him off to work with a cheerful smile, but on any given evening, he might walk through the door and not greet me at all. I felt invisible, hurt, and confused. Sometimes we sat at the dinner table without a word between us.

I felt punished by his silence, and my frustration and anxiety began to get the best of me. I was determined to make him explain himself. I wasn't going to be ignored. If he refused to engage with me, I got louder, as if he were deaf. During my outbursts, he gave me a strange, smug smile, like he enjoyed seeing me lose control. I couldn't think straight, and for the first time, I wondered if he had driven his wife crazy.

I was a yo-yo on his string, pulled to him one minute and pushed away the next. I thought of every possible reason for his behavior. Had something gone wrong at the office? Had I done something wrong? He wasn't shouting or hitting things, but I almost wished he would. Being ignored was the worst form of rejection.

During this time, his father became quite ill. Putting aside my unhappiness and confusion, I stayed close by his side. We came home late one night, exhausted and grieving after sitting with his father at the hospital. We were both asleep when I heard our miniature pregnant poodle scratching on the kitchen door.

She wasn't near her due date, and although the weather was cold outside, she had a doghouse in a small enclosed area at the back of our home. She wasn't unprotected, and I ignored her at first. But when she began to whimper and cry, I immediately got up to let her in. My movement woke my husband.

Physically drained and worried about his father, he gruffly said, "Don't humor that damn dog, and don't bring her in here. I need to get some sleep."

Out of respect for him, I lay still and drifted back to sleep.

Early the next morning when I opened the door to let her into the house, five lifeless puppies were lined tightly against the door. The mama poodle was beside herself, licking them and trying to push them into the warmth of the house.

The puppies were cold and limp. I gathered them up and held them against me as I rushed into the house. I turned the bathroom wall heater on high and wrapped them in a towel. I rubbed them, and the little mother licked them, but to no avail. She was making the most pitiful, frantic sounds trying to save her babies. When I knew our efforts would not revive them, I rocked their little bodies, crying hysterically.

Something broke in me, something I had locked up for years. When my husband left the house, I wailed. I didn't even realize at the time that those baby puppies triggered something I had never allowed myself to feel—grief over the death of my own children.

And when there were no more tears to cry, I pulled myself up off the bathroom floor and got busy cleaning the house. I turned my attention to my marriage and work. More than ever, I wanted to recapture those early happy days with my husband. One night, I came out of the bedroom waving a little white handkerchief in surrender, trying to bring some levity to the situation and declare a truce. "Could we talk?" I asked.

He looked up but didn't answer.

"Would you please talk to me?"

The same man who had been so cold and withdrawn for months put his face in his hands and wept. "I've been ashamed to tell you, but two months ago, I was fired. I had a lot of debt when we married. I didn't tell you, because I thought I could keep up the payments, but I've gotten behind, even on the mortgage. I know your practice is just beginning, and you can't handle the bills. There's no way out of this. We have to sell the house. Can you forgive me? Please?"

I was almost relieved. The embarrassment and stress of his financial predicament explained his strange behavior. I took him in my arms and said, "Of course I forgive you. We'll figure this out together." I thrived on helping people, and he needed my help.

I worked tirelessly, taking on extra hours every chance I got. We moved from our comfortable house into a small apartment. The romantic husband I'd married was back, and so was our drinking. The alcohol truly seemed to make things better.

I wish I could say things normalized in our marriage, but my husband never went back to work. I was working nights and weekends while he was sitting at the same bar where I met him, trolling for his next wife/paycheck. He had been spending money on other women the whole time we were married. I don't know if I was angrier with his deceit or with myself for being so easily seduced by charm and good looks.

A third divorce—I was mortified. An especially shaming remark from my mother summed up what I thought about myself: "I can't imagine why anyone would come to you for therapy."

I feared that very thing. If my patients knew about my struggle with depression and my poor track record in relationships, why would they engage me as their therapist? But they *didn't* know, and amazingly, my practice grew. My patients felt better and made better decisions. When people walked out of my office, I often wished I could be my own therapist.

16

40 Days

From the depths of despair,
O Lord, I call for your help.
Psalm 130:1

Demeaned by another failed marriage, I felt pretty low. I didn't even have my own place. I was renting a room in a friend's house, and that would turn out to save my life. I was taking anti-depressants, but I needed more to help with discomforting anxiety and insomnia. My psychiatrist prescribed Xanax and warned me that the drug was highly addictive. "Take only as prescribed."

Some nights, it didn't put me to sleep. But if I mixed just a little wine with the Xanax tablet, I slept like a baby through the night. Over several months, I gradually took more and more of the calming drug. When the doctor refused to re-fill my next prescription unless I took the medication as directed, I thought, *No problem, I'll follow directions.*

But it was a problem. The prescribed amount left me feeling even more anxious. It didn't matter that it was a legally prescribed drug. I was hooked. I needed more for the desired effect.

I told myself the same thing I'd told many clients: *You only have so many chances in this life, and you're doing a good job of using up all the ones you have. It's time to decide once and for all that you will do whatever is necessary to create a healthy, sane life. You can't make rational decisions abusing mood-altering drugs. Sobriety has to come first.*

I vowed to beat the addiction. With determination but no medical supervision, I took the matter into my own hands. I flushed the Xanax pills down the toilet. Once they swirled out of sight, there was no turning back. Quite proud of this new climb toward health, I settled in bed with an excellent novel to enjoy the evening. If only I had been reading Barbara Gordon's book, *I'm Dancing as Fast as I Can,* I would have been warned that I was about to descend into the hell of *benzo* withdrawal.

I couldn't seem to get comfortable and concentrate on the words I was reading. I changed positions but couldn't lie still. My body had a mind of its own and began to twitch and jerk. I hurt all over. I took a warm shower, but I needed something more. A shot of Scotch whiskey took the edge off the discomfort for about two minutes. The second shot barely made a difference.

My nightshirt was wet with sweat, but then I would shiver with a chill. Out of the corner of my eye, I saw something run up the wall. At first, I saw only a few tiny creatures, but they quickly turned into an army of spiders. Somehow they got under the covers and were crawling on my legs. I scratched and thrashed about in bed, shaking too much to stand up and get away from them. I was screaming, but I didn't hear myself. I was lost in a world of psychotic drug withdrawal. My roommate called 9-1-1.

The emergency room staff smelled alcohol on my breath but didn't know if I was drunk, crazy, or both.

Realizing I was close to a seizure, a nurse plunged an Ativan-filled needle into my arm, and the shaking stopped. I also lost consciousness, so I couldn't tell them what I had done. When I finally woke up the next day, I tried to explain how I ended up in the ER.

The hospital staff didn't quite see my valiant attempt at drug withdrawal in the same positive light as I did. They recommended immediate transfer to a highly touted treatment center—the kind of place movie stars go for rehab. The glowing description of the former dude ranch in the clean desert air sounded like a heavenly way to escape my troubles—divine enough to dole out a big chunk of cash to get through the door.

I imagined leisurely veranda chats with other patients as I watched the sun slowly drop in the western sky. Since this place cost more than a five-star European vacation, I anticipated gourmet dining and an attentive compassionate staff. Mostly I wanted to nap and recover from my harrowing experience. I packed my swimsuit, several escape novels, and the book about alcoholism given to me at the hospital. I was sure I wouldn't need it.

When I arrived at the ranch, I was met with the sign Expect a Miracle on the front gate. I sure needed a miracle. With this positive thought in mind, I entered the facility.

When I got inside with my many pieces of luggage, everything abruptly changed. They confiscated every article of clothing, all reading material, and every kind of cosmetics I had packed. Now dressed in a hospital gown, slippers, and a blue lab coat, I was escorted to my room.

I was enraged. I was treated like a street junkie. When the door closed, I wondered if I was locked in. *What papers had I signed? Had I given up my rights?* Right then, I decided I was in the wrong place. But where was I going to go? If this place didn't work, I would be out of options and out of money. I would rather kill myself right on their front steps than get my hopes dashed again.

After losing everything I brought with me, including what was left of my dignity, I learned I was under close supervision in a detox unit. With no place to hide and too sick to run, I lay mute for several days, wishing I would die. Rock bottom was no damn fun. I was down for the count, never dreaming it was the best thing that would ever happen to me.

To the best of my recollection, I stayed alone in the detox room for about four days. It was the last time I would be alone for forty days. When I had the strength and stability to move out of detox, I was shown to a plain double room and was handed a packet of many stapled pages. These pages turned out to be my daily schedule and a long list of single-spaced rules and regulations.

In addition to many daily meetings, I was to take turns cleaning the bathroom I shared with another girl, make my bed every morning, and do my own laundry. I was quite ticked off that they didn't provide maid service. Would a movie star put up with this? I couldn't ask, because there wasn't one in sight.

I felt more like an inmate than a patient. My time was tightly controlled. The schedule was exhausting: morning and afternoon lectures, individual and group counseling, numerous psychiatric tests, and required evening attendance at twelve-step meetings for specific addictions. It turned out that they defined almost every behavior as an addiction, and in their opinion, I was addicted to just about everything under the sun.

Patients were allowed no caffeine, nicotine, television, magazines, or phone calls. The rules removed every distraction to help us examine our history, behavior, and feelings 24/7. They said they had seen miracle after miracle if people followed their program.

On practically every inch of wall space in the facility, a large sign displayed the twelve steps, discussed *ad nauseam*. The first three steps stated that we needed God. Those steps were so objectionable that after the church experiences, I thought there would be no way to get past them.

- Step One: We admitted we were powerless over alcohol—that our lives had become unmanageable.

- Step Two: Came to believe that a Power greater than ourselves could restore us to sanity.

- Step Three: Made a decision to turn our will and our lives over to the care of God, as we understood him.

No, no, no, and hell no! I was so furious I threatened to sue the facility. I could go to church for free and hear the same load of bull they were serving up. I admitted that my best efforts had gotten me where I was, but I wasn't defeated or humble enough to accept what they offered. I still had the misplaced belief that I could handle my life, and no one was going to tell me what to do.

While the other "inmates" were laughing and joking and praying, I was pouting and balking. I overheard them talking about getting down on their knees, morning and night, to ask God for help, and I thought, *No way*. But I did have to admit they seemed "happier" with every passing day.

No bright light or any other kind of great spiritual revelation made me decide to get on my knees the twelfth day I was in treatment. I finally considered, *If this is working for them, might it work for me? It seems ridiculous, but I've tried being a vegetarian, fasting, dancing, meditating, and so many other things, why not try this? I've been halfway around the world seeking answers, what do I have to lose?*

Embarrassed to be seen on my knees talking to an imaginary God, I hid in the large walk-in clothes closet every morning to perform the charade. Feeling foolish and fake, I repeated the words they gave me to say. I didn't believe for one moment that anyone was up there listening. Thirty-three days after I drove through the "miracle gate," I got down on my knees and said the same words I had been reciting every morning: "God, I'm powerless."

The moment the words left my mouth, a wave of sweet relief washed over me and took my stress and struggle right out to sea. I inhaled deeply and experienced the stillness of peace. Contentment settled around me like a warm, soft blanket. Something soothed my soul like never before. Was God the one soothing me?

Did admitting I was powerless open the way for him? Feeling powerless was an unexpected relief. I wanted to believe there was someone I could count on. Even if I couldn't depend on God, the recovery community was there for me.

One week after the momentous closet event, the staff pronounced me a miracle, even if it had taken forty days, and their usual treatment program was only twenty-eight.

Now I didn't want to leave. I had found something in the desert I didn't want to lose. I bargained for more time, fearing that my old loneliness was waiting for me and could cause me to relapse.

The treatment team told me I never had to be lonely again. If I attended meetings, I would meet people who would provide a better support system than I'd ever known. They were people who understood addiction and the pitfalls of early sobriety—men and women who had fought and won the same battles. Someone would be available 24/7.

All that sounded good, but the idea of going around town announcing I was an alcoholic and prescription drug addict stopped me in my tracks. I had done everything possible to hide my problems. I had a reputation to uphold. Thankfully, the fear of relapse overcame my foolish pride, and I heard myself agreeing to attend ninety meetings in ninety days! As we drove through  the outer gate to the treatment center, I saw another sign bidding me farewell: You Are a Miracle.

The promises and steps of Alcoholics Anonymous provided a lifeline and a blueprint. As explained on pages 83–84 in their "Bible" fondly called the Big Book, I am told that:

"If we are painstaking about this phase of our development, we will be amazed before we are halfway through. We are going to know a new freedom and a new happiness. We will not regret the past nor wish to shut the door on it. We will comprehend the word serenity and we will know peace. No matter how far down the scale we have gone, we will see how our experience can benefit others. That feeling of uselessness and self-pity will disappear. We will lose interest in selfish things and gain interest in our fellows. Self-seeking will slip away. Our whole attitude and outlook on life will change. Fear of people and economic insecurity will leave us. We will intuitively know how to handle situations which used to baffle us. We will suddenly realize that God is doing for us what we could not do for ourselves."

I still almost gritted my teeth every time I heard the word *God*, but I saw others reaping the promises declared in the book. Almost without noticing it, I changed too. I didn't know I could have so much fun without alcohol. Our group went out to eat, played charades, watched movies, and celebrated significant milestones together. I felt known, liked, and even loved. We were like one big family.

Most people I met in AA were generous, honest, and open. They willingly sacrificed their time and energy day or night to help an addict in trouble. It was the Christian commandment to "love one another" in real-time. I made strong, intimate, nonsexual friendships with men who cared for me but didn't use me—the kind of relationships I had wanted.

When a feisty seventy-four-year-old "broad" became my AA sponsor, I found the mother I'd never had. She was warm, affectionate, available, and tough as nails. In the first year of my sobriety, we attended hundreds of meetings, but our relationship went far beyond the meeting room. We spent hours working through each of the twelve steps, laughing *and* crying. She helped me face my behavior head-on and make amends where necessary.

After a year of sobriety, I was *allowed* to date. The most hilarious adventure Millie and I ever took was a trip to the grocery store to buy condoms (just in case I needed them one day). As we read the various pros and cons, we bent over with  laughter. Eventually, everyone in the grocery store who came near us was laughing too. What was this seventy-four-year-old woman doing in the condom aisle?

When Millie's eyesight failed, she had to hang up her car keys. I was privileged to shop for her and drive her to meetings, but she was homebound and alone most of the time. Not once did she ever express loneliness or fear about being blind. She wasn't lonely, because she had a best friend who was with her all the time.

That friend was Jesus. He was as palpable to her as I was, and she could sense his love and closeness. She told me that he loved me too, but she never hit me over the head with Christianity. She loved me right where I was. I'm sure she prayed for me to know Jesus, but she never told me about it if she did.

To members of a recovery group, it doesn't matter how many mistakes you've made. You are welcome. Even if you showed up drunk, you would probably be offered a cup of strong coffee and a listening ear.

I found a Benevolent Higher Power in those groups. It was a relief to acknowledge that there was a power greater than myself. I saw him work in the lives of people in AA, not in a church building. If churches rallied around people like AA, the world would be a better place.

It seems when drunks and addicts gather together in search of sobriety, a Benevolent Power is right there with them. If God is love, I met him through the people who walked alongside me on the road to recovery. When things got lonely, frustrating, sad, or just dull, I asked God for help, and a light appeared in the darkness.

My life was sober, sane, and settled. I spent many contented days in a small rental house, rising with the sun to walk through the quiet neighborhood in the fresh morning air. I quit smoking, lost weight, and made new friends. I was getting physically healthy, and I was proud of myself for making good choices. TA had worked at one time, but now AA was the plan.

17
Incurable

Have compassion on me, Lord,
for I am weak. . . . I am sick at heart.
How long, O Lord, until you restore me?
Psalm 6:2–3

The first few years of recovery were the best years of my life. Sobriety and the steps gave me a plan to follow and helped me reach important goals. Everything was positive and hopeful.

My practice grew, and I purchased a large house with a home office. I loved decorating every room, having small dinner parties, and hosting recovery gatherings with many new friends. I met a handsome, sober, financially successful man, and the relationship looked promising. Feeling content, not wanting for anything, I relaxed. It was the best of times.

And then . . . it was the worst of times. Tragedy struck and kept on striking. When my younger "adopted" daughter was diagnosed with lung cancer, I flew to her side. When I entered the hospital room, her biological mother was there. It was challenging to meet the mother who had allowed her young daughter to be abused and then abandoned her, but I could see the pain and regret in her face. She hadn't been in her daughter's early life, but she was there now. She stayed by her side through every day of the terminal illness. On the next trip to see my daughter, her mother and I began calling her "our girl."

Just weeks later, my kind and gracious aunt was murdered in a heinous home invasion. I rushed to my cousin's side and tried in any small way I could to help her deal with this shocking and enormous loss. To this day, I am amazed at how she coped with the evil in this event. It was because of her faith. She knew she would see her mother again, and she was determined to carry on her legacy. Soon after my aunt's burial, my uncle, who never recovered from the stress of the robbery and his wife's death, also died.

Abdominal pain sent my father to the doctor for a colonoscopy. Unfortunately, the colon was perforated during the procedure, resulting in emergency surgery. The following morning when he sat up, he suffered a debilitating stroke.

The colonoscopy revealed he had both lung and colon cancer. It was more difficult for him to accept his paralyzed side than cancer invading his body. He was fighting the restraints and alternately raging and crying. Nothing had ever controlled him before, and he wasn't about to give in if he could do anything about it. There seemed to be no way to console him. He was so determined to escape his limitations that he refused any cancer treatment. Six weeks later, he was dead.

Two weeks after that, my beloved Millie and my cancer-ridden thirty-nine-year-old adopted daughter died within days of each other. Five people I loved had died in five months.

For months I experienced severe fatigue but thought, *Who wouldn't be exhausted with the schedule I'm trying to maintain? My exhaustion is an entirely normal emotional reaction to so much grief.* Endowed with my father's grit and determination, I kept telling myself, *Just do the next right thing.* The AA slogan, *one day at a time*, kept me going.

There was no time to grieve and recover before the next tragedy struck. I didn't make time for meetings, and gradually I relied on the old *I-can-do-it-myself* survival mode, which would inevitably fail.

One morning, I just couldn't get up. I went through a litany of reasons for my lethargy: *I need more sleep, need to eat better, need to exercise, need a meeting, need to increase my antidepressants.* Doing any of those things would probably have helped, but the only thing I did was reach out for more psychotropic medication. The right mixture of meds was the fastest remedy.

Because of my drug-abuse history, the doctor hesitated to prescribe for me. "I don't want to overlook any physical condition that might be causing your symptoms. I want you to have a medical checkup, and then we can discuss it. I also want you in therapy and meetings." He may have saved my life.

I begrudgingly visited the internist, who ordered routine blood tests. I thought I might be anemic at the very most and was irritated at the psychiatrist for requiring me to have the appointment.

Within days, the medical office lady called. "The doctor wants you to make an appointment. There are some irregularities in your lab results."

I still didn't suspect any serious medical condition and scheduled the follow-up appointment.

In his office, the doctor explained that the lab tests revealed highly elevated liver enzymes. Several possible conditions needed to be confirmed or eliminated. "You need to be hospitalized so I can perform a liver biopsy."

Whoa! That seemed very serious. There must be some medication that could get me on the mend. The doctor gave me no choice. "You have to have this biopsy," he said.

The biopsy confirmed that I had an auto-immune disease that causes the body to attack itself. Any organ, including the skin, could be affected, and my liver was probably already compromised due to excessive alcohol use. I got my wish for medication all right—four prescriptions, including steroids.

The doctor also prescribed rest and water therapy to maintain mobility. The nurse handed me pamphlets about a disease called Lupus, and I walked out of the building shocked and scared.

Initially, it didn't occur to me that I wouldn't overcome the disease. I had pushed through every obstacle, every tragedy, and the consequences of every grave mistake I had ever made. This was just one more thing to overcome—like any other challenge.

I was determined to do whatever I needed to do. For over a year, I doggedly struggled to maintain my independence. Almost everything I had learned about powerlessness and needing support from others seemed to have gone out the window.

After being hospitalized with a nasty lung infection, I had to face some hard facts about Lupus. The lungs are often the first place the disease attacks. My liver had already been affected, and now my lungs were being scarred. As the weeks went by, I became increasingly ill and realized that I might not get well.

It took eighteen months of laborious paperwork to get disability income from Social Security. I was forced to sell my large house. It wasn't just a *house*—it was the home I independently created for myself when I turned fifty. I sold what furnishings I could and moved into a four-room apartment.

Even in this small space, I could barely function. My self-sufficiency came to a screeching halt. If it hadn't been for my executive assistant who, despite a reduced salary, stayed with me and helped with groceries and other essentials, I couldn't have continued living alone.

Being forced to stay in bed isolated me and resulted in a deepening depression. I was forced to cancel plans over and over, and relationships ended. When I stopped working, I lost the purpose that gave my life meaning: I couldn't help others. I couldn't help myself.

I couldn't wish, cry, or deny the illness away. I felt the most unattractive of all emotions: self-pity. Seeing myself as a victim was deadly. I knew that, but I couldn't stop worrying. Those long hours in bed gave me plenty of time to worry. *What would become of me? How sick would I get? What would happen when I simply had no more money? Where would I live?*

As my disease progressed, the doctor eventually said a word I will never forget: *incurable*. The thought of death haunted me. For someone who had danced with death on and off for most of her life, the romantic idea of dying young should have come as a welcome relief. But I wanted death on my own terms, quick and easy. This disease caused *long* suffering. Suicide could have ended my despair, but another word hijacked my mind and scared me more than the word *incurable*. That word was *Hell*, and it was preceded by another terrifying word: *sin*.

Afraid to live with the suffering ahead, but afraid to die and suffer eternal Hell, I panicked. I knew one thing for sure: my name was not written in that Book of Life. And I doubted I could get my name in there, especially when I had been so mad at God.

Was being mad at God the unforgivable sin?

The Glory Years

18
Surrounded

Righteousness goes as a herald before him,
preparing the way for his steps.
Psalm 85:13

It was a lonely Christmas week, and most of my neighbors
were on vacation or busy with family and holiday activities.
I had been out of food for several days, but I had no
energy to leave my house. I wished I could just die of
starvation. I was tired of being sick and feeling helpless. I
hated being dependent on other people. I wanted out of
my miserable life, even if I was going to Hell.

When the phone rang, it was a friend from AA. Her
friendly voice said, "Need anything from the grocery?"

"Yes, thanks. Some soup would be nice." I guess I did
want to live one more day or I wouldn't have answered the
phone.

My friend and her husband dropped by like little
Christmas elves. They stocked my fridge, shared a warm
bowl of soup, and made a request: "May we pray for you?"

Abruptly I said, "Hell, no!"

A bit taken aback, they asked, "Why?"

"Because I'm not on speaking terms with Jesus."

123

After that exchange, they quickly left.

After they left, I chastised myself. *That was rude. That couple went out of their way to feed you, and you practically kicked them out of the house. You should have let them pray.*

Concerned about my health, but even more concerned about my attitude toward Jesus, they probably prayed as soon as they closed their car doors. They didn't need my permission there. Unbeknownst to me, they returned to their church and challenged them to pray me *into the Kingdom.* Many of those church members bowed their heads or lifted their eyes toward heaven and sincerely prayed for me to be physically healed or *saved* before it was too late.

A few days later, this same woman called again. "It's Christmas, and you need to get out and see the Christmas lights, and then we'll have some dinner."

To my surprise, the word *yes* fell out of my mouth again. Immediately, I regretted it. *What was I thinking?* It was like Siberia outside. I hated cold weather, even when I was healthy. I struggled to shower and dress, and then I heard the knock on the door.

The car was toasty warm when I got in. They even brought a pillow for my comfort in the cramped back seat of their compact car.

We drove through the mega-mansion part of town, and the lights were amazing. I enjoyed looking at the lawn displays and opulent decorations. No street lights were needed in this neighborhood. I wondered what the glow looked like from an airplane.

I expected we would dine at a nearby restaurant, but they drove away from the city. I was tired and a little irritated. "Where the heck are we going?"

"We want you to meet some of our oldest and dearest friends. They really want to meet you, and we promised we would bring you to dinner."

I should have been suspicious. *Why would these friends want to meet me? Darn it! Why did I go out with them?*

We finally arrived in a nice neighborhood in an adjacent town. When we entered the home, Christmas lights twinkled from the decorated tree, and stockings hung above the fireplace. Seven seemingly ordinary people were casually chatting in the kitchen.

Shortly after introductions, we gathered around the dining room table. Dinner was a long, boring affair filled with superficial chatter, and no one seemed interested in getting to know me. Nothing about this entire fiasco made any sense.

After dinner, I hoped we would say our goodbyes, but we moved from the table into the comfortable living room. The room was quiet. Suddenly, I felt extremely anxious. My heart pounded as I tried to reason with myself. An alarming mental picture formed in my mind. This circle of strangers was going to tighten around me until I had no air to breathe. I wanted out of that house.

I'm sure only a few seconds passed before the husband of the house spoke into the silence. He looked directly at me and asked, "How did you and Jesus get on such bad terms?"

I was startled out of my fear. Shock turned into outrage. The motive of my so-called friends became crystal clear: I had offended them when I refused their prayer, and now they had me cornered.

To my embarrassment and dismay, I began to weep. I could only stop sobbing long enough to get out some of my experiences with Christians and churches. I shared the terror I experienced as an innocent four-year-old the first time I attended church and how unjustified condemnation fell on me as an adolescent. When I read in God's Word that he regretted ever creating the human race and would destroy it, I turned away from Christ and the Church.

My audience didn't interrupt. They didn't ask a single question. They waited for me to empty out everything I needed to say. Some in the circle wept quietly. I wondered why they were crying.

When I fell silent, the man spoke. "We are part of a small home church, and as Christians, I am apologizing for the church people who made you feel condemned in the name of Jesus. I know I speak for the members of the group when I tell you how sorry I am that this happened to you."

Others joined in, saying, "Yes, some Christians are misguided. Their actions are wrong."

The husband said, "I believe God is grieved when children are hurt in his name. We are heartbroken for you, heartbroken that you have lived without the comfort of knowing Jesus. He wants to be your closest friend. I imagine you feel lost and alone."

His last words were accurate.

"Is it all right if we pray for you?"

The moment he finished speaking, frightening pictures flashed through my mind again. The people morphed into a flock of devouring vultures, and I was their prey. Just as suddenly, an ocean wave threatened to pull me under and suffocate me. What was happening? Where were these thoughts coming from? I wanted to bolt to safety, but I was trapped.

I hadn't given my consent, but a person touched my shoulder. Like magic, my fear began to melt with her compassionate, gentle touch. Being encircled still felt a bit weird. As they laid their hands on my head and shoulders, they spoke a strange language. *Was I involved in some kind of pseudo-Christian cult ritual?*

Even with trepidation, I experienced a sense of safety that was totally unexpected. I was relieved to let my guard down. This experience was similar to being on my knees in the closet of the treatment center.

Something extraordinary was present in this place, but I became anxious again as they continued to pray. *For crying out loud, finish praying, and let me go home.* Suspicion crept in. *What did they really want from me?* And why did the idea of dying at the hands of these people keep coming into my mind? Finally, I heard the amens and breathed a sigh of relief. We all got up from where we were sitting. Each person hugged me and asked God to bless me. We found our coats and headed for the car.

On the drive home, it was quiet for some time. I broke the silence. "Obviously, you and your friends think God is good and loves everybody, but that has not been my experience. I felt compassion from your friends and heard some new things tonight, but one small group of people doesn't wipe away the hurt and fear of a lifetime. If God is the Father of Creation, I think he could have done a better job. I have a few things I'd like to say to him—a whole list of complaints I'd like to make."

They nodded and didn't try to talk me out of what I thought. When we arrived at my home, they came in and helped me get to bed. I felt tucked in, like a child. And then they went on their way.

I had a long, deep dreamless sleep. For the next few days, I had to admit I felt more peaceful. *Nothing had changed in my condition or circumstances. Did this new feeling come from the Christians? Was there some truth in what they said?* I wasn't about to get my hopes up, because I didn't have the comeback-kid determination to overcome another defeat.

Less than a week later, the same woman called for the third time. Now what? Excitedly she said, "I found a way for you to share your list of complaints with God."

Good Lord, I thought. That expression surprised me, and I'm still surprised I didn't just hang up the phone. Instead, I said, "What way? What are you talking about?"

She related that her church was sponsoring an eight-day workshop called the Barnabas Journey. It was an opportunity for people who had conflicted feelings about God to get resolution and peace. I would be welcome to join about fifty people who attended her church.

Was she crazy? First of all, I didn't think Christians had any conflicted feelings about God. Second, I'd heard about seminars where they lock you up in a room for days at a time. No way!

A bit sarcastically, I asked, "Do you think I'm going to willingly be stuck in a room with fifty Christians? For eight days? Have you lost your mind? You'll never convince me this is a good idea."

She didn't argue. "Just pray about it."

Now I was expected to pray. What next?

I tried to put it out of my mind, but I couldn't. I longed for peace as I never had before. For many months, I'd been worrying about the damaging effects of stress hormones on my body. I was convinced it was partially responsible for my illness. The toxic chemicals released by my anger toward God and fear of Hell were flooding my body with *poison*. I would never get well as long as I was so reactionary. I longed for peace as I never had before. My life could depend on it.

My feelings bounced me around like a ship in rough waters. One minute I was the four-year-old child who had been terrified by the pastor's words, and the next minute I was the defiant teenager who vowed never to enter the doors of a church again. In reality I was a desperate, discouraged fifty-five-year-old woman who didn't know where to turn next.

Could the workshop possibly help resolve some of these issues? What or who was Barnabas? What would that group of Christians think of me when they heard my opinions? And what about God? Was he going to show up at the hotel?

I had no intention of becoming a Christian, but I didn't want to be so angry every time I heard God's name. I wrote in my journal that I wanted to make peace with God. I didn't know that I had written a prayer, and I certainly didn't realize that God was listening. But something made me decide to take the Barnabas Journey.

19
Mercy

When you are suffering all these things, you
will finally return to the Lord your God and
listen to what he tells you. [He] is a merciful
God; he will not abandon you or destroy you.
Deuteronomy 4:30–31

I'd never been more apprehensive. What strange force had over-taken my brain and volunteered me to stand before the fire-breathing God of my youth? *Come on,* I told myself, *You're over-reacting. You can do this.*

I kept walking toward the ballroom of a local hotel. With each step, my heart pounded faster and harder inside my chest. I wondered if I might stress myself into a heart attack.

Why was I so afraid? I wasn't in physical danger, but I knew all too well that ridicule and condemnation could hurt even more than being hit. *What will those God-believers think of me? How will they treat me?* I reminded myself, *You're no stranger to condemnation. You can handle what people think. But what is God going to think?*

When I entered the cavernous room, I was told to leave everything at the door, sit in the interlocking straight-back chairs, and be quiet. The leaders were abrupt and certainly intended to control the other sixty-five people and me sitting obediently in silence. Everyone else seemed calm, but I felt like a sheep being led to slaughter.

The heavy double-doors closed with a decisive thud. I surprised myself by muttering, *God, I'm sorry.* I didn't realize those words were a prayer of repentance. Tears began running down my cheeks before a word was said.

A long line of workshop leaders stood at the front of the room. They introduced themselves and warned us that we would only get out of the workshop what we put into it. After informing us that the next few days could change our lives, the room plunged into total darkness, and Gloria Estefan's voice filled the room.

Her words described a woman searching for a way to "come out of the dark." Finally, love would bring her into the light. I related to every word that described the searching. *Would I ever make it out of the dark?*

The room suddenly filled with light, and I observed that almost everyone was crying. *What were these Christians crying about?* The long week had officially begun.

For the first few days, we heard lectures that were more psychological and philosophical than religious. None of the information was new to me, and I was getting a bit impatient. I knew the God stuff was coming, and I wanted to get on with it.

During almost every session, some tear-jerking song was played, obviously designed to tug at my emotions. The days stretched far into the night, and slowly but surely, the process brought me closer to the history of my family and my experiences with God.

The leaders were kind and caring, tenderly helping me face the betrayal and abuse I felt from my family and the church's condemnation. They were sad that I wasn't treasured by my caregivers who had convinced me that I was unlovable. They were critical of church experiences that made children believe they were sinful and unforgivable. Those false beliefs had almost been too much for me to bear. Not one person in the group condemned me in any way.

"You're not bad. You're just a human being," they said. "Without God's help, life is too difficult for any of us to live well." *Who was this helpful God they spoke of? I didn't know him.* I was face-to-face with the issues that brought me into this room, but the session was over. There was no opportunity to ask questions or reiterate my beliefs about the absent, judgmental God I knew. It was time for lunch, but I was so troubled I couldn't eat a bite.

When we returned to the meeting room, I was chomping at the bit to speak, but the lights went out as we were seated. Another song filled the air. But this song would change everything.

The words were meant to be reassuring, sung by a father (God) to his child. "I was there when you gasped your first breath, and my arms opened wide when I heard your cry." What? God was in the room when I was born? His arms were open wide? I certainly wasn't aware of his presence then, and I had never felt his arms around me in my whole life. I felt a pang of sadness.

But what this *God* sang next made me livid. He said he heard my first prayer and listened to every promise I ever made. If these words were accurate, it meant God listened to every trembling plea for forgiveness, every heartfelt commitment to be good, every desperate prayer for help, and did nothing. He allowed me to suffer torture day and night, filled with guilt and fear, knowing I blamed myself for every failure. I was the bad girl who couldn't be good, the little girl told she was a deep-down-filthy rag. He never showed up to contradict my beliefs or ease my pain.

The last words of the song, "You will always be a child in my eyes, and I still hold you close," was more than I could hear. The words may have comforted other people in that quiet, dark room, but I felt cheated and fit to be tied. My voice split the quiet of that room, bursting into a repeated, "No! No! No! That's a lie!"

The little girl in me, who never felt loved by God, wanted to accuse this God of being unfair and cruel. If he was such a good Father and loved *all* his children, why the hell hadn't he taken care of me? He let me be abused by my family and the church. He let me feel so alone in the world where I wanted to die. The worst thing is that he could have prevented it all, and he did nothing.

The group leaders were prepared for my explosion— almost as if they expected it to happen. The lights switched on, and two chairs sat facing each other in the middle of the room. An older man sat in one chair, and I was led to the other. This man was going to play the role of God, and I was given permission to direct all my questions, pain, and confusion at him.

I hurled accusations at him, constantly asking, "Why? Why?"

He responded with patience and understanding, "I see your pain and confusion, but you *are* my *beloved* child. I have loved you every day of your life. I know it's hard for you to believe my words right now, but today can change everything you believe. If you let me come into your heart, your eyes will open, and you will see the truth."

I nearly gagged—everything this old man said infuriated me. I didn't trust a syrupy word that came out of his mouth. Pie-in-the-sky clichés weren't going to solve my problems. I continued my protests.

So, Mister God, are you finally going to show up after all these years?

Are you going to heal my broken heart?

Are you going to heal my disease?

Are you going to absolve me from my sins?

Are you going to let me into Heaven, if such a place even exists?"

The man playing God took no offense. Instead of anger or disgust on his face, I saw only sorrow. But I didn't care. Jesus was a man, and my heart and mind were locked against the silver tongues and sweet words of men. Even if these were the words of Jesus, they didn't penetrate my hard heart. My wall of distrust was thick and unyielding. I hung on to my unspoken mottos:

Never surrender.

Never trust anybody.

Never get your hopes up again.

The thought of unlocking the protective wall around my heart and trusting any man sent a shiver of fear through my body. But I was so tired of fighting. When I finally had no fight left in my body and no words left to say, I sat in stony silence.

But he still had a lot to say. He spoke in a quiet reassuring voice. "If you can admit how much you wish you had a father, it will open your heart. In all your searching, in all your waiting, you have never found an answer. Let me take your fears. Let me take your sin. You will not be punished for anything you have done, because Jesus paid your debt on the cross. He came to save you,

134

and when you accept his sacrifice, you will know you are forgiven, and that you can rest in his arms."

His words tugged at my heart. *No punishment? Forgiven? Saved? Peace? Rest in the arms of Jesus? Could any of this be true?* I didn't know it, but his words turned the key in the lock to my heart just a tiny bit.

He went on: "If you accept Jesus as your savior, he will be waiting for you when this earthly life is over. You will live in Heaven, where you will never shed another tear or know a moment of pain. Your body will be transformed into perfect health. If you believe my words, your uncertainty will be over. I will saturate your heart with everything you have longed for: unconditional, never-ending love, joy, and peace."

I knew I was at a life-or-death crossroad. Would I choose this new life or continue struggling toward inevitable death? The man in the chair made it sound so easy—just believe and receive. It wasn't easy. I had a bastion of defenses. Surrender would not come quickly. The struggle was intense, but eventually, I didn't care how it ended. I just wanted it to end.

Exhausted, I slumped over, my face in my hands. There was no sound in the room but my own weeping. An unfamiliar warmth began to surround me. And then I saw that the room had filled with light, even though my eyes were closed. I sensed the presence of power and gentleness. I knew it was Jesus.

It made no rational sense whatsoever that the King of the entire universe wanted to be near this dirty, sniveling mess of a woman. Was this the time of judgment I had long feared? My sin and shame bent me even lower. Should I fall at his feet and beg for mercy?

No, he didn't want that. I imagined he lifted my chin so I could look into his face. Kindness and compassion were all I saw there. And then, he extended his nail-scarred hand to me. Surely God Almighty didn't want this unclean hand in his.

The warmth of his limitless love melted my doubts and fears. I reached out. The man across from me clasped my hand in both of his. Everything in me changed in a flash. All the tension and struggle left my body. My cells felt transformed and energized. My mind was clear and at peace. Had I been healed?

I did not want to open my eyes. I was afraid the experience would end. But I did open my eyes, and the presence of God still felt very near. I'd thought God was done with me ages ago, but I was so wrong. He had been waiting for me to feel his touch.

As hopelessly lost as I was, only a dramatic expression of God's love could have penetrated my defenses and made me believe he existed. I'd attempted to alleviate my shame in a hundred ways, but until he adopted me and changed my name to Worthy, my efforts were futile.

I had not gone to him willingly. God came to me and took me in as his daughter. The searching, the hurting, the waiting was over. In surrender, I won everything and lost only what needed to go.

From one minute to the next, I shared a common inheritance with the other participants. It seemed as if every one of them gave me a big hug. I not only had a father, but I also had sisters and brothers, all of us heirs to God's eternal promises.

If someone had asked me earlier in the day what a conversion experience looked like, I would have described it as a scene from *The Ten Commandments* movie (the Charlton Heston version). The convert would triumphantly and blissfully walk down the aisle of a magnificent cathedral, maybe wearing a white flowing robe and even a veil. Tears of joy would stream down their cheeks as they went forward to meet their bridegroom, Jesus. Organ music would fill the sanctuary with glorious melody, and the brilliant light of God would shine through stained glass windows.

I had to laugh at my ideas. I was a disheveled, messy sight when I met Jesus. He wasn't looking for a cleaned-up, white-robed, Sunday-morning-smile woman. He wanted a woman like me. And now I knew he would never let me go. I thought I would be blissfully happy, content, and unworried forever.

20

Goodness

*I am confident I will see the Lord's goodness
while I am here in the land of the living.*
Psalm 27:13

Within the hour, little doubts pestered me like annoying
gnats. I've got to hand it to Satan; he's as slick as they
come. His most deceptive ploy is to convince people that
neither he nor God exists. I had been in his clutches,
believing his lies since childhood, but he was unseen and
unknown to me. He had owned my life, and now he
wasn't going to give me up without a fight.

He was the one whispering those troubling thoughts in
my ear: *Do you think this high is any different from all the rest?
Do you think you have actually met someone called God? Remember
all those other times you thought you'd found the secret to happiness?*

My mind was flooded with some of those other times
and places. Meditating in the Athenian Temple of Delphi
in Greece, I imagined the oracle had given me the answer
to living peacefully—just focus on simple things. That
sounded easy enough. It wasn't. I could focus my
attention span on some object for about five seconds.

I met the chill of dawn on Paradise Island, twisting my body into yoga positions called *asanas* on a wooden platform built over the ocean. As the sun warmed my body, I did feel peaceful—for about five minutes. I danced euphorically to sitar music in the Rajneesh ashram. I didn't have a care in the world—as long as the music played. There were card readings and astrology charts and trips to new-age centers in Mexico and beyond. As hopeful as I was that each new path would bring the desired change, the peaceful state never lasted. The moments were always temporary, often dissipating before I reached the airport and never staying very long after I walked through my front door and back into ordinary life. The thrill was gone. Nirvana always seemed out of reach.

Would my experience at Barnabas turn out to be another temporary Cloud Nine?

I returned to my apartment, physically and mentally exhausted from eight emotional days. Everything looked the same. I dropped my suitcase by the door. On the way to bed, I noticed that some kind person had watered the plants. A week's worth of mail was stacked neatly on my desk. Everything was in place, but the atmosphere was strangely different.

I felt a presence that had never been in my home before. I can't explain it, but I knew I was not alone. I longed to understand these new feelings. I wasn't familiar with the promise in Exodus 33:14, where God said, "My presence will go with you," but I sensed he was there.

The moment I believed God was real, that he had created me and was my Father, I was spiritually born into a new family. Like every other baby, I needed to learn my Father's language. Two thousand years before, Jesus inspired his followers to write down the lessons I would

139

need. The words they wrote would stay alive, and I would live by them (2 Timothy 3:16; Hebrews 4:12; Romans 15:4). I came to know God's character through their words.

At the moment my identity changed, I inherited a list of incredible gifts. I didn't deserve any of them, and I certainly hadn't earned them. Nothing in my world had ever been so generous and grand as God's unlimited benevolence. Even though I had rejected him, even hated him, he never stopped loving me. I had been his enemy, but rather than the punishment I expected, he loved me and forgave me.

As I look back, the blatant lies I believed about God's condemnation and the sparse information I had about his goodness were staggering. Had I only known *how wonderfully kind, tolerant, and patient God is; that it was his kindness that would turn me from my sin* (Romans 2:4), I would have known it would be the Lord's invitation that brought me to him. I would never be driven to him out of fear and guilt. It was God's written word that constantly reassured me.

- God bought my freedom at a great price and then joined his Spirit with mine and adopted me as his very own child. He reconciled me close to him (Galatians 4:5; John 1:12; Romans 5:10; 8:16; 1 John 3:12).
- He gently opened the lock around my heart. I had a new heart, a new mind, and a new life. I also received the shield of faith to protect that heart and a helmet to protect my thinking. God provided every protection from the enemy that we needed. (2 Corinthians 5:17; Ezekiel 11:19; Ephesians 6:10-17).

140

- The almost incomprehensible gift is that Christ came to Earth knowing he would take on my sin and yours. He willingly died a painful death to pay our debt for those sins. God sacrificed the Son he loved for you and for me. *But God shows his love for us in that while we were still sinners, Christ died for us* (John 3:16; see also Romans 5:8; 1 Peter 3:18).

- Our father does not punish us as we deserve, but in his unfailing love, he removes our sin as far as the East is from the West. He forgave my every sin and threw them far away (Psalm 103:10-14; Luke 7:48; 1 John 1:9; Romans 8:1-2).

- He promised me that nothing could ever take me away from him (John 10:29; Romans 8:39).

- He placed hope in my heart that I count on every day (Hebrews 11:1; 1 Peter 1:3; Romans 8:25; Titus 2:13).

- He gave me the Gift of Faith, the assurance that I can trust him. By grace I was saved through faith. (Hebrews 11:1; Ephesians 2:8).

- He gave me the Holy Spirit to live in me as my comfort, teacher, and guide (Acts 1:8; John 14:26; 1 Corinthians 6:19; 1 John 2:27; Ephesians 1:13-14).

- He endowed me with spiritual gifts that enable me to complete his plan in my life for the common good of all (Romans 12:6-8; 1 Peter 4:10-11; 1 Corinthians 12:4-7).

- He will never leave me nor forsake me (Hebrews 13:5; Joshua 1:5; Deuteronomy 31:6; Psalm 27:10).

- He gave me the ability to live in peace, no matter what happened in my life (John 16:33; 2

Thessalonians 3:16; Isaiah 26:3; Colossians 3:15; Philippians 4:6).

- He gave me the desires of my heart and the ability to overcome old cravings (Psalm 37:4; Romans 6:33).
- He gave me the ability to help others know him. I became royalty, holy, a priest, and an ambassador (1 Peter 2:9; 2 Corinthians 5:20).
- He will heal me emotionally and physically, instantly or day by day (Psalm 147:3; Jeremiah 30:17; James 5:15; 1 Peter 2:24).
- He promised I would never die. I will live with him forever (John 3:16; 10:28; 14:2).
- One day he will wipe away every tear, and death shall be no more. No more crying or pain of any kind (Revelation 21:4).

If you don't know him, these words may seem like pie-in-the-sky and syrupy sweet. I don't know how else to describe him but with my own experiences. He's a good, good Father, and his goodness changed every moment of my life.

He wasn't Santa Claus, giving me everything my little heart desired, and he didn't prevent challenges. He gave me the things I *needed*, not necessarily what I *wanted*. I'll never know the many times he turned me from the wrong way or protected me from harm that never touched me. When things seemed to go wrong, I didn't always see his purpose immediately. My trust grew when I realized over and over that he was working in the background. His hand was on my life. With new eyes, I clearly saw what I could never have seen before.

For many weeks after Barnabas, I cozied up to newfound contentment, especially enjoying the first fruits of the Spirit—love, joy, and peace. I spent my days resting on my sofa bed, since I still couldn't make it up the stairs very often. Christian praise music filled my apartment. I watched preachers on obscure television stations that I never knew existed. I was quite happy in my insulated little life, but I was isolated from other Christians by my illness. I knew God created us to be part of a body.

I was about to find out how beautifully God provides for us. He sent a real live *angel* from the church mentoring program right to my house. She arrived weekly with her Bible and baked goodies. She and those sweets filled my apartment with the aroma of Jesus. We studied Scripture, and her kindness and faith taught me about being a part of the family of God.

Through the French doors of my den, we watched rain, sun, and snow as every season passed. We studied and laughed and cried like the sisters God created us to be. I took my homework seriously and absorbed God's Word for many hours every day.

That first year of my walk with Jesus was incredibly full of rich, different information—and more sisters. I was welcomed into the fold by a group of older church ladies, the Go Girls, who invited me to join their monthly supper club. Another group, The Followers, invited me to join their weekly prayer group. These gals were not the stuffy sisters I had expected. We sang and laughed until tears streamed down our faces. We prayed for one another, celebrated life's special events and shared moments that only God could have orchestrated. They helped me grow my faith in record time. They also taught me to pray boldly—and if needed, loudly.

When I didn't feel well enough to drive, one of them picked me up or the whole group detoured to my house. More than once, I met with these dear ladies in my pajamas. When a tambourine was placed in my hand during a songfest, I found a new rhythm and a new biblical directive: "Praise him with the tambourine" (Psalm 150:4). I loved my joyful new life.

The day of my baptism was a public declaration that my life was surrendered to the one true God, that I would follow his teaching to the best of my ability, and that I had been reborn into the family of God, who really could wash away the pain of the past. It was especially sweet to be baptized by the woman who had walked me through meeting Jesus in Barnabas. God knows just the people we need. Now I was really ready to follow the

great commission to "make disciples of all nations, baptizing them."

The more I learned about the truth that set me free, the more I wanted to tell others. God had taken a selfish, grieving, empty, fearful woman and made a born-again, sold-out, Bible-reading, praising, praying-on-my-knees, Jesus-loving woman. He used my circumstances to bring me to the end of my old self. In my new identity, I wanted to give back.

Ephesians 2:10 clearly states that he creates us anew in Christ Jesus, so we can do the good things he planned for us long ago. I was ready to do those good things.

The same missionary zeal he gave me forty-two years earlier resurfaced, but I was too weak to leave my apartment for any length of time. I didn't understand why God hadn't completely healed me and sent me out as his ambassador. After all, I'd been studying for a whole year. I watched Joyce Meyer, James and Betty Robison, and T. D. Jakes on TV, read the Bible, attended church when I could, and prayed.

I was chomping at the bit to be a hero of the faith and had no idea that the enemy could use my best intentions in misguided ways. I thought, *Now that I'm saved, I'm good to go.* Satan was dusting off my old I-can-do-it attitude and trying to send me out on a mission before I was prepared.

This book is not about Satan, but I mention him here to suggest that he was behind my frustration (John 10:10). He hates all Christians, and new Christians are the most susceptible to his wiles. Even though he can't defeat us, he'll do his darn level best to distract us and distort the truth of Scripture. I used to laugh at people who thought Satan existed.

I don't laugh about Satan anymore. He is a formidable foe. He is the Father of Lies (John 8:44). When I didn't have God's armor, his lies affected my life so dramatically that I didn't want to live. Until I was adopted by God and knew the truth of his Word, I listened to Satan and unknowingly spread his lies to others.

For fifty-five years, Satan had convinced me that I was unworthy and going straight to Hell. Now, that relentless liar was telling me I was a *superstar*. If the devil can't slow us down, he'll speed us up.

Although my motives may have been good, even godly, Satan was seductively pumping up my ego. He's good at convincing us that we can set out with pride, grit, and determination, earning full credit for whatever good thing happens. The fact is that whatever we accomplish is the result of the gifts, purpose, and talents bestowed upon us by God.

God saw Satan's scheme, and he was not about to let him lead me astray. God would use every one of my life experiences, with every tear combined with the abilities he had given me to minister to others. He would increase the fold in powerful ways, but not yet. Romans 15:4 comforted me: *The Scriptures give us hope and encouragement as we wait patiently for God's promises to be fulfilled.* God's timing for our future is always perfect. Had I been physically healed too soon, I would have followed Satan's seductive plan.

I needed steeping in the cup of God's love and hearing his still, small voice as he prepared me for his purpose. He is a tender God who often whispers. Too sick to go and

146

do, I grew to know him at a deeper lever through the sacred time of rest and study he was providing.

But the devil was always there, wanting me to doubt that the Lord was satisfied with me just sitting around. One day as I was fretting, I imagined Jesus was standing right behind my chair. I physically leaned back on him like John leaned on him at the Last Supper. Sometimes, I think I hear his actual voice, but at the very least, my thought was this: *You are my child in whom I am well pleased.* He gives me peace and reassurance when I need it.

21
Purpose

***God causes everything to work together for the
good of those who love God and are called
according to his purpose.***
Romans 8:28

As the months rolled by, my daily routine was watching
Joyce Meyer's daily sermon on TV, reading the Bible, and
singing rousing worship songs. I was content in my
newfound peace and joy and hardly gave any thought to
physical healing. After all, I had an incurable disease.

But one day, I woke up with a strange thought. *I don't
feel sick.* I speculated. *Maybe I just had an excellent night's sleep.*
But day after day, I kept waking up with new energy.
Gradually, I noticed that I could go a little farther on my
morning walks. I stopped taking a nap during the day. My
playlist invited me to put a little pep in my step while
doing chores and making meals.

I had come a long way from a wheelchair, and the joy
of the Lord had, indeed, become my strength. I could be
at church services every Sunday and eagerly read the
bulletin to see what events I might attend during the week.

I no longer needed the high dose of steroids I had been taking to keep going, and I wanted to share this exciting news with the rheumatologist. The doctor was skeptical but agreed to perform the necessary lab tests to determine the status of my disease. A week later, I received a call from the same office where I had received such a dire diagnosis a few years before: "The doctor would like you to make an appointment."

I have to admit, I thought the news might not be what I wanted to hear. *Did I believe in modern-day healing? Were those symptom-free days a temporary reprieve?*

When the doctor walked into the examining room, he smiling. Holding the test results in his hand, he said, "There are no lupus antibodies in your bloodstream."

We sat in silence for a few moments.

"You mean I'm not sick? I don't have lupus?"

"No, you still have lupus. There's no known cure for this disease, but you are in remission."

"Do you believe in healing, Doctor?"

"Well, there are things we don't understand that may look like healing."

Every second I sat there, I was more confident I had been healed. I pressed on: "I think Jesus healed me. Do you know Jesus?"

"I'm Jewish," he said.

I had to chuckle. So was Jesus. "Doctor, I was Jewish too, but Jesus is called the Great Physician. The lab results validate that we've seen him at work."

He smiled patronizingly, patted my shoulder, and went on to see other patients.

Not only did I have spiritual strength, but now I had physical strength too. I was like the woman who had been persecuted by Satan for years (Luke 13:11-13). My

149

compassionate healer had restored me to health. Thank you, Jesus! Praise the Lord!

I was finally ready—mind, body, and spirit—to embrace the missionary zeal God gave to me as a young girl. He was going to take every misstep I ever made and turn it into good for others. On my very first mission trip, God used my former addiction (bad news at the time) to shine "his good light" on a group of Russian pastors struggling with the rampant spread of alcoholism in their country.

You've read my recovery story. You know that when I was first introduced to God through the steps of AA, I almost turned away. How ironic that now, I was certain these same steps would help the pastors depend on the One who could heal them. They could possibly influence thousands of Russians, including the pastors themselves, who were dying in the streets from this disease.

In a meeting of about 100 people, with the help of a very competent translator, I stood humbly in the center of a vast ballroom, sharing with the audience that I was saved from alcoholism by a powerful, loving God. I invited anyone suffering from alcoholism to join me in the center of the room, and twenty people accepted my invitation. Then I asked anyone who had a family member suffering from alcoholism to come forward and stand with us. Another fifty people came. When I said, "If you personally know and care about someone suffering from this disease, please join me," almost every person in the room came to stand with us. We locked arms and stormed Heaven in prayer for God to lift the curse of alcohol abuse from them, their friends and loved ones, their congregations, and their country.

I continued teaching through the conference, and in every meeting. I felt inexplicably drawn to a young man in the audience. There was something about him that compelled me to know him better. His journey—born to a mother in jail and now living homeless on the street—is a story worthy of being told. After I returned to the United States, I couldn't get him off my mind.

Through the pastor who brought him to the conference, I supported his move from the cold street into a boarding house.

Thanks to Skype, email, and Western Union, I have extended a true mother's heart to him for the past twenty-one years. He became my first son. I have returned to Russia to visit him, and we are in almost daily contact. Being his "adopted mum" is a great gift and privilege.

Around the same time as my trip to Russia, I met a young woman in Dallas. From our first meeting, we realized that we had suffered similar wounds in childhood. Those experiences gave us a sense of understanding and closeness. We enjoyed many of the same hobbies, and a lovely friendship began. Soon I met her husband and their four boys. The whole family welcomed me into their lives, and we started attending church together. I had *adopted* others, but now I was about to get *adopted*.

One Sunday after church, I was attending a planning meeting for an upcoming church retreat. The oldest boy slipped into the room and handed me a sealed envelope.

151

Soon after that, the second oldest did the same, followed by his two younger brothers. When I got to my car and opened the envelopes, I found Grandmother's Day cards. My heart swelled as fast and big as a helium-filled balloon.

 As soon as I arrived home, I pulled out my colored pens and stickers and wrote a letter to the boys: *Am I your Adopted Grandmother? If so, let's all sign on the dotted line and make it official.* From that day on, I was Grannie Annie. I had always been a deeply lonely person, and God places the lonely in families (Psalm 68:6).

Through our church outreach, I met a group of Sudanese refugees. I was horrified to learn that as children, they witnessed their families' massacre, and their villages were burned to the ground. The male family members were slaughtered. The women were taken as slaves or raped and then murdered. Most of the children who survived were eight to twelve years old and often carried their younger siblings. They were alone, hunted day and night by wild animals and predator soldiers. They had no clothing, shoes, food, or water. Only one in ten survived their thousand-mile trek to safety.

Beverly Parkhurst Moss, who became my "comrade-in-arms" to help the Sudanese women, was so touched by their survival story, she authored a book about their ordeal: *Dark Exodus: The Lost Girls of Sudan.* If you don't know the lost boys and girl's story, I recommend reading her book or watching the movie, *The Lost Boys of Sudan* (2003).

After languishing in a refugee camp for years, they found themselves in the United States, some with their own young children. They had never seen a stove or a toilet, slept in a bed, or ridden in a car. The women were not given the benefit of an education, and some barely spoke English. Living in such a complex society was quite confusing, and they needed every kind of help.

Amazingly, God brought my life full circle. All those years ago, when I watched joyful African children dancing on a rickety projection screen, I was willing to go anywhere on the globe to be God's missionary. But God had a plan for the African children and me all along. He brought Africa to me.

To this day, I have the privilege of being "Mama Anne" in the Dinka community. One particular family of six girls thinks of me as their "grandmother." When a new baby in the family was named after me, it was a great honor.

Many of these young women, even though they could not read or write when they arrived, love this country so much. They studied and studied and memorized the material to become citizens. We are astounded at their accomplishments. And all along the way, their unwavering faith in Jesus inspired us.

There is no logical explanation for why one particular homeless man touched my heart so deeply. Like most others we met in the community, he had witnessed the loss of his entire family. He was subscripted to serve in the Sudanese Liberation Army and was wounded in battle. Because of his physical condition and emotional trauma, I don't think he would have made it on his own. He was drowning in despair, poverty, and drugs. He needed every kind of practical help, but mostly he needed to know he was not alone. He needed a family.

My adopted family and I helped him with medical needs, housing, and food, and we loved him fiercely. And we were privileged to witness a miracle. We watched God change his life. He got sober, left the streets, joined the church, was baptized, and had a home of his own.

I have to admit that I watched over him like a mother hen, and we certainly made an interesting mother and son pairing. I am short and chubby with white hair and fair skin. He was a skinny, over-six-foot man with the inky-black complexion of the Dinka tribe.

Five years ago, Michael's life ended due to a medical mistake. His death was a terrible shock and loss, but it comforts me to believe that God needed him in Heaven to tend his herds of cattle on a thousand hills. The Sudanese have been herdsmen for centuries. Michael didn't find peace this side of Heaven, but

154

he is with God and his beloved bovines now.

Mama was a word I thought I would never hear when I aborted my babies and sterilized myself. And yet, like the barren women in Isaiah 54:16, God removed the shame of my youth and told me to enlarge my house for all the spiritual children he would send me.

> *Sing, O childless woman, you who have never given birth . . . for the desolate woman now has more children than the woman who lives with her husband, says the Lord.*
>
> *Enlarge your house; build an addition. Spread out your home, and spare no expense! For you will soon be bursting at the seams. . . . Fear not; you will no longer live in shame. Don't be afraid; there is no more disgrace for you.*
>
> *You will no longer remember the shame of your youth and the sorrows of widowhood. For your Creator will be your husband; the Lord of Heaven's Armies is his name! He is your Redeemer, the Holy One of Israel, the God of all the earth. For the Lord has called you back from your grief—as though you were a young wife abandoned by her husband," says your God.*

Of all the blessings God has showered on me, my children are the greatest gift. And God wasn't through with me in the Mama department. Fifty years after the fact, I was led to the Someone Cares post-abortion recovery program. Although God had forgiven me, I had never forgiven myself.

With the group's love and understanding, I went through the gut-wrenching stages of guilt and grief that I had been afraid to feel all those years ago. Even so, I thought the grief would swallow me, but I found myself soothed by Jesus' love and forgiveness and the kindness of the group. Toward the end of the process, we were invited to name our children and write letters to them. We chose the day they would have been born to celebrate as their birthday if we desired. In a ceremony called *Remembrance*, the children we never held in our arms were honored.

In my imagination I can see my Abbie and Jake playing in Heaven. I fully believe they were joyfully taken into the waiting arms of their loving Father, and one day I will hold them in my arms forever. God is so kind to let me see this picture.

I have shared my redemption story in prisons, churches, and women's retreats to help other women bring their broken hearts and guilt to God.

I take no credit for any of the ministry opportunities God provided to me. And I take no credit for my gifts in this area, because they were given to me by God for his purpose. He uses this broken-but-healed woman to tell his story of glory. God has done it all. If you need to hear his voice, I pray you will read his message through the words of this book.

22

Forgiveness

Forgive anyone who offends you.
Remember, the Lord forgave you, so you
must forgive others.
Colossians 3:13

Like the unfinished emotional healing around my abortion,
I had other issues that needed to be confronted. When
one becomes a Christian, God forgives their past, but they
may have work to do.

As a child, I needed a savior to protect me from my
mother's illness. My father was not the best person for the
job, but no one else volunteered. He was my hero and sat
on the throne of my hopes and dreams as surely as any
god. Up until the time I started seeing boys as a teenager,
he was my "everything."

He came crashing down from his throne when I
realized that being his chosen companion was
inappropriate and had complicated every relationship I
tried to have with another man. Current psychology would
define the relationship with my father as romanticized
emotional incest. A more popular term is *spousification*.

The time I spent close to him helped me avoid my mother's rejection and made me feel wanted. We both tolerated her anger rather than acknowledge that there was a problem needing medical intervention. Her behavior didn't look like mental illness. She just seemed mean, cold, and jealous. She suffered something she wouldn't overcome alone.

My father didn't hurt my mother or me deliberately. I don't think he had any idea how his *love* for me would affect both of us, but the repercussions of his behavior confused me about men for most of my life. I tried to forgive him many times, but because he never changed his behavior, the reprieve never lasted. Once I had loved my father above all else, but for years I avoided him.

When he suffered a massive stroke, I put my feelings aside, booked a flight, and flew to his side. At the doorway to his hospital room, I was shocked at the sight of a disheveled old man in the bed. He wasn't the proud, handsome man I had known. He was struggling against the restraints that held him like a wild stallion and was uttering garbled words as tears ran down his cheeks.

My hand flew to my chest. Momentarily, I couldn't get my breath and had to step into the hallway, out of sight. I was overwhelmed with sadness, compassion, and pity for this broken man. I knew he didn't want to be seen in his condition. I wasn't sure I could go back into the room and keep my composure.

My ability to compartmentalize got me through the next few days. This man wasn't only my father. He was a dying man who needed kindness. I held his hand and wiped his spittle and tears with the compassionate detachment that health-care workers use to do their job.

At times, memories broke through my denial, and I saw the man I had loved with all my heart as a little girl. When that happened, the grief was so gut-wrenching, I went to my car and wept. But just as frequently, other flashbacks made me leave his room in a fury.

I wasn't a Christian when my father became ill. Try as I might, I didn't have the grace of God to forgive him. Those last days passed slowly and without healing. My father had his resentments too. Although he never spoke of it, I am sure it was a slap in his face when I changed my surname. There was a chasm of unspoken pain and disappointment between us. Although this was obviously the last opportunity for reconciliation, neither one of us reached out to the other.

When he died, I longed to put all memories, good and bad, into the grave with him. I want to be completely free from him. Late at night before he was laid in the ground, I went to the funeral home alone. The guard allowed me into his viewing room. The lighting was dim. The entire building still and quiet. The scent of the many flower arrangements threatened to suffocate me. The elaborate, hand-carved casket stood open.

Dressed in his horse-racing silks, he looked very much alive. Those silks stirred up too many memories of years we spent together at the fair. Instead of establishing some kind of peaceful finality between us. unwanted anger surged through my body.

I went there to say, *Daddy, I love you, and I forgive you.* But the words would not come. With grief and remorse, I put my hand on his chest, looked down at his face, and spoke my truth. "I cannot forgive you. You cost me too much." I turned and walked out, with all that had happened between us still within me.

The next morning, I arrived at the house I grew up in, to escort my mother into the black Lincoln limousine that would take us to the funeral service. I walked up the same steps where I used to sit waiting for my daddy every night. My mother was sitting at the kitchen table in comfortable pajamas, drinking a cup of coffee.

Shocked, I blurted out, "Mother, why aren't you dressed?"

She looked directly at me. "I'm not going. You sit in my place. You've always been there."

Somewhat in shock, I returned to the limousine, drove to the funeral home, and sat in my mother's seat as her husband of fifty-seven years was memorialized and buried. The speakers repeatedly directed remarks to "his wife of many years," even looking in my direction. Didn't anyone realize she was not there?

As a young girl, I saw my father's affection like *the best thing that ever happened to me.*

As I grew older, I realized that although he may have never intended it, his charming ways controlled and manipulated me. After I realized the effects of our relationship, I protected myself from his words of affection by keeping my distance and constructing a thick concrete wall around my heart. I locked it with a large key and began to think of my father as *the worst thing that ever happened to me.*

As I began to write about my father on the pages of this book, God gently and frequently convicted me to forgive him and count the blessings I had received from him. I was like him in so many ways—outgoing, charismatic, affectionate, animal lover, with the confidence

160

to accomplish difficult things with excellence, and grit and determination.

I asked God to unlock my heart and let me forgive and love my father with no defenses. The Lord didn't break through the wall around my heart using condemnation and shame. Instead, he gently used the key of love to open the lock. He didn't disavow anything about my father or his behavior. Instead, he opened my eyes to see that he had created my father as one of his precious children. But the child lost his way and became a broken man. No matter what my father did or didn't do, God always loved him.

When the truth of who my father was entered my heart, tears ran down my cheeks. Genuine compassion overcame me, and I gladly forgave the man who had been my daddy. God freed me from a heavy burden.

When I consider my father's adamant anger toward all things Christian, I believe he must have suffered a great disappointment. Maybe like me, he felt judged and condemned by people in the church. Maybe he felt he was never good enough and gave up. I still cry from time to time, wondering what hurt my father so deeply.

After I forgave my father, I wrote him a letter. It was long overdue, and I wish I could have given it to him when he was still alive. Our words have the power to heal or to wound. I wish I had helped my father heal.

> *Dear Daddy,*
> *I tear up as I write that name. I haven't called you that in a very long time.*
> *I grieve for all we missed, because neither of us had the help of Jesus. We loved each other the best we could.*
> *My deepest prayer is that you turned to God in your last days and that you will live in his perfect love forever.*
> *I love you, I forgive you, I place you in God's loving care.*

It is to God's glory, not my human ability that I forgave my father.

23
Heaven Bound

If you confess with your mouth that Jesus is Lord and believe in your heart that God raised him from the dead, you will be saved.
Romans 10:9

And there was still the residue from the strained, painful relationship with my mother. As her Alzheimer's disease progressed, she became confused, fearful, and childlike. For a moment, I was able to be close to her.

I sat close to her, and we giggled together, watching old comedies on TV. When she was frightened, I held her hand and reassured her. I tucked her in at night and helped calm the agitation she often felt.

Our sweet time was short-lived when, like many Alzheimer's patients, she became combative and suspicious. She needed help so desperately, but she turned on me when I tried to help.

What a lonely and dark life she had, and now she couldn't escape the memories of the past. Her suffering was so apparent, I asked one day, "Mother, is there anything, anything at all, that I can do for you?"

163

Her answer was a strident, "Yes! Bring me a gun so I can kill myself." Had she been able to acquire a weapon, she may have joined her sister in taking her own life. It seemed nothing on this earth had ever lifted her darkness.

It was before dawn when the shrill ring of the phone broke through my sleep. Early-morning phone calls are rarely good news. The nurse's voice was kind but deliberate. "Your mother's breathing has changed. This is usually a sign of the end. I think you'd better come now."

Fumbling to dress as quickly as I could, I knew this might be the last chance I would ever have to tell my mother about Jesus.

When I asked Christ to be my Savior, he forgave me and adopted me, and he gave me those beautiful feet I heard about and wanted as a teenager. I never thought I could forgive my mother, but Jesus took away the resentment that filled my heart and replaced it with compassion and understanding. I longed to give her the opportunity for salvation.

It would be my finest hour serving God if I could introduce her to the only Light that could save her. I prayed fervently for courage and composure to present his message boldly and kindly. *Dear God, I know my mother's place in Heaven does not depend on me, but please put the words in my mouth and soften her heart to receive the truth.*

The minute I entered her room, I went right to her bed and turned on the light. Her eyes were fixed as if she was looking far into the distance. I don't know if she even saw me. Her mouth was locked open in a silent scream as if an unseen enemy had frightened her. My mother, a woman who had hated being overweight all her life, now weighed only ninety pounds.

I raised the bed so I could look directly into her eyes. I placed a pillow behind her rigid neck and took both her hands in mine. She looked right at me. I spoke quietly but deliberately: "I love you, Mother, and I have something so good to tell you."

I thought, *Oh, Mother, I pray for you to understand these critical words. This is the most important message I have ever given to anyone.*

I spoke kindly and slowly, as I would talk to a child who had never heard the salvation story. "I want to tell you about a man named Jesus. Although he is the Son of God and lived in Heaven, he came down to Earth because God and Jesus knew we needed to be rescued. Even though God sees all our mistakes and sins, he loves us just the same. Out of his love for us, God let Jesus die on a cross to pay the penalty for our sin. The good news is that God raised him from the dead, and he lives now with his father in Heaven. If you believe in Jesus and ask him for forgiveness, you'll go to Heaven to be with Jesus forever when you die. I'll be there too, because I believe in Jesus.

I want you to be there with me. If you repeat these words in your mind and ask Jesus to be your Savior, I promise he will hear you. Just follow along with me:

> *Jesus, I believe you are the Son of God.*
> *I believe you died for my sins.*
> *I have done so many things wrong, and I am sorry.*
> *Please come into my heart and forgive me. I want to follow you home and live in your Kingdom forever.*
> *I love you, Father.*

My mother never blinked. She never took her eyes off my face. I believe she heard me. I think she expressed a belief in Jesus and that we will be together again to have a relationship that was never possible on this earth.

After we prayed on what was supposed to be the day of her death, Mother miraculously rallied for a few days. I asked her to forgive me for shutting her out of my life. I assured her that I forgave her for everything that ever happened in our conflicted relationship.

Then she slept and slept and peacefully slipped away. I was not there when my mother died, but I know God was. I believe he tended to her lovingly as she passed from the dark of her life into the Light of his love.

$\mathcal{E}$ 24 $\mathcal{B}$
A Time to Dance

You have turned my mourning into joyful dancing. You have taken away my clothes of mourning and clothed me with joy, that I might sing praises to you and not be silent. O Lord my God, I will give you thanks forever!
Psalm 30:11-12

There was another area of my life that needed tending. I was paralyzed by fear of repeating past behavior. If someone had suggested I might be looking for God by dancing the night away in some dark, smoky bar, I would have laughed out loud. And if you'd told me Satan was using dancing to lure me into sin, I would have sarcastically quipped, "Give me a break." Moving in sync with a man's body made me feel connected and desirable. My touch hunger was temporarily filled, but those nights, combined with alcohol, inevitably led to danger and regrets.

When I became a Christian, God filled the emptiness left by past rejection and failed relationships. For the first time, I recognized the things I had substituted for real love. Even so, when I was invited to go dancing with my new Christian friends, I was afraid to take the chance. What if dancing triggered a desire for something beyond the dance floor? I always declined.

When this fifty-six-year-old grandmother heard about a workshop called Dance to the Lord, I was intrigued but thought to myself, *They're dancing in the church's sanctuary? Is that even allowed?* Ecclesiastes 3:4 clearly says there is a time to dance, but was this the time and place?

I accepted the invitation with some trepidation, still fearing that dancing might trigger yearnings I wasn't ready to face. At the beginning of the day, the pastor shared Bible verses describing dancing as a form of worship and praise (Psalm 149:3; 150:4). He mentioned that some churches saw any form of dancing as evil, but others joyfully celebrated God's goodness by dancing to and for him.

God could take the way I had used my body so wrongfully and turn it into something that honored him. With the pastor's sweet words in my ears, I entered the softly lit sanctuary. Soothing worship music played in the background. I could feel the tension begin to drain from my body. What a pleasant surprise.

But then the pastor uttered the same words I heard in the Rajneesh ashram. "Close your eyes and let your whole body respond to the music." I was jolted into the memory of dancing myself into a frenzy in a room full of strangers. Satan attempted to steal my joy with that unpleasant memory and bind my body right there in the church sanctuary.

But God wouldn't let that happen. It was like he whispered quickly and quietly: *Your body is sacred to me, and I made it to give you pleasure. It is right for you to enjoy it. I'm glad you're here. Come dance with me.*

At first, I stood absolutely still. I couldn't move. Even with God's words anointing me with permission to come alive, I was frozen. I lifted my eyes and hands toward God, believing he was looking down at me, inviting me to enjoy my body. I felt a mix of reverence, wonder, and childish joy. I dropped to my knees, fully submitting and waiting for him to take the lead. After a few moments, I felt lifted up. I was laughing and crying at the same time.

I bowed low to my dance partner. Everyone and everything in the room disappeared. I danced for God's eyes only and gave no thought to my appearance or my dance moves. Unashamedly, I was physically expressing my love back to the One who loved me. Embraced by God's love, I found what I had desperately searched for on the barroom dance floor.

25

Wonderful Merciful Savior

The Lord your God is living among you.
He is a mighty savior. He will take
delight in you . . . He will rejoice
over you with joyful songs.
Zephaniah 3:17

I love the Scripture stories about God calling unlikely, ordinary people like me to fulfill his purposes on Earth. When other people encouraged me to write my story, I felt unqualified. But I wanted to tell others about the God who changed every thought in my mind, healed my body, and filled me with faith and hope. But did I really have the words?

All the years before I accepted God, I saw myself as unworthy and unwanted. I even changed my last name to Worth, but I remained trapped in the muddy pit of despair, guilt, and depression. God longed to lift me out of the darkness, but shame and humiliation wouldn't let me receive his light.

He was always waiting, just a decision away, waiting and wanting to love me. He will wait close by until the last breath for every person. It comforts me to believe he was

170

there with my mother and father in their final hours. He doesn't want one soul left behind.

Ultimately, the most vigorous efforts of the enemy couldn't hold me back from stepping into the cleansing light of God, who rescued me and breathed new life into me. I was a new creation with a new mind, a new heart, and a new name—Worthy Daughter of the King.

I don't think it would be fair to only tell you about the glory side of my life after I met Jesus. Once saved, we are still free to choose the good or the bad, the blessing or the curse, the choices that lead to life or the actions that lead to our death. And we are choosing, whether we know it or not.

God offers us inner peace, joy, and love. But there is one who roams the earth determined to defeat and ultimately destroy us. His name is Satan, and he wants to tempt us away from God and the abundant life Jesus died to give us. Scripture calls him the father of lies, deceiver, accuser, evil one, liar, tempter, and murderer (John 8:44).

Once we know Jesus, Satan cannot possess us, but he can torment and tempt us. He disguises his dark offers very well. He lures us through the "lust of our eyes," distracts us through discord in relationships, tricks us with pride, and devastates us with shame. He will use anything and anybody in any way at any time to steal our joy.

He offers all kinds of delicious substances and activities that will make you feel better—for a while. His temptation for you might look like a big piece of iced chocolate cake, an X-rated movie, an opportunity to steal, or swipe right on your phone. Everything Satan offers is counterfeit love, leaving you more empty than you were before.

Because I didn't know he existed, I had no defense against his deception. I was ignorant of his wiles and temptations, unaware that he was whispering convincing lies in my ear. Without God's protection, Satan nearly succeeded in killing me. When Jesus taught us to pray, he reminded us to ask the Father to protect us from Satan: "Lead us not into temptation, but deliver us from the evil one."

Even though we need protection from the dark forces of evil while we are on the earth, God owns the Kingdom and has the power and the glory forever. Satan attempts to distort the truth about God, about us, and about the future, but God provides armor against our foe (Ephesians 6:10–18). Satan has been defeated, but we can be wounded by the cunning tricks in his war arsenal until we are in Heaven.

- If he has made you believe God is judgmental and vengeful, keeping track of all your sins of imperfection, you've fallen for one of Satan's most damning lies. God loves you the same way he loved Jesus, and nothing you ever do will make him love you any less. He understands your weakness. (John 17:23; Hebrews 4:15)
- If you think God has condemned you, you are hearing the voice of the enemy. There is no condemnation for those who love the Lord (Romans 8:1). The Lord is patient and slow to anger (2 Peter 3:9).
- If you think God abandoned you and never saw your pain, he wants you to know he was there (Hebrews 13:5).

- If you think you have done too much wrong in your life and are unforgivable, know that your Father in Heaven wants to forgive you and let you know that you are as precious to him as the prodigal son (Luke 6).
- If you feel beyond hope, it's because the enemy wants you to feel that way. Hope deferred makes your heart sick (Proverbs 13:12).
- If you think the saving of your soul is of no consequence in Heaven, Scripture tells us there is rejoicing in the presence of God's angels over one sinner who repents (Luke 15:10).
- If you think it's too late for you, that you've gone too far for God to want you, remember how he transformed this old gal into a new person. I will never see the gates of Hell, because God saved me. When this life is over, I will go to live forever in my Father's house, the mansion of true forever love. Jesus went there to make a place for me (John 14:2).

One of our best defenses again Satan is to keep our mind filled with God. We have the Holy Spirit dwelling within us who will guard and direct us. God has power over Satan and the world, and if we ask for his help, we are under his protection.

If I listed a thousand adjectives in an attempt to describe what it's like to be in God's presence, the words wouldn't come close to the actual experience of walking in the light of his love. I was a broken-hearted child in need of a father's comfort. His limitless love filled up every empty space in my being and put a song in my heart. He didn't use big words when he spoke to me as his little daughter:

You are my beautiful daughter.
I have loved you from the moment of your conception, and
I have never stopped loving you for even one moment.
I am always here when you need me.
I enjoy you, so come close to me.
Nothing will ever change our relationship.
My promises are forever.

If nothing gets one iota better in my life, I am content. I trust that God will work out every situation for the best for all concerned. He is a good God, and there is a purpose in everything that has happened and will happen in my life. How do I know these things are true? Because God bestowed me with the gift of faith, and by faith, I believe all the promises in the Bible.

Born again, we are adopted into the royal family of God, the living King, Creator of the Universe, who is Omniscient, Omnipotent, Omnipresent, Immutable, Righteous, and more. Despite his majesty and power, he encourages us to call him by the simple name Father. He wants every child he created to be close to him. Of all the words used to describe his attributes, I love to call him Abba, my Daddy.

Scripture Verses

I've done my best to tell you about this mighty but tender God in my own words. But in case you are not familiar with scripture or may not own a Bible, I have listed the verses I consider most important for you here.

Chapter 19

John 14:27 — I am leaving you with a gift—peace of mind and heart. And the peace I give is a gift the world cannot give. So don't be troubled or afraid.

Psalm 27:8 — My heart has heard you say, "Come and talk with me." And my heart responds, "Lord, I am coming."

Hebrews 4:16 — So let us come boldly to the throne of our gracious God. There we will receive his mercy, and we will find grace to help us when we need it most.

Chapter 20

Exodus 33:14 — The Lord replied, "I will personally go with you, Moses, and I will give you rest—everything will be fine for you."

2 Timothy 3:16 — All Scripture is inspired by God and is useful to teach us what is true and to make us realize what is wrong in our lives. It corrects us when we are wrong and teaches us to do what is right.

Hebrews 4:12 — *For the word of God is alive and powerful. It is sharper than the sharpest two-edged sword, cutting between soul and spirit, between joint and marrow. It exposes our innermost thoughts and desires.*

Romans 15:4 — *Such things were written in the Scriptures long ago to teach us. And the Scriptures give us hope and encouragement as we wait patiently for God's promises to be fulfilled.*

Galatians 4:5 — *God sent him to buy freedom for us who were slaves to the law, so that he could adopt us as his very own children.*

John 1:12 — *To all who believed him and accepted him, he gave the right to become children of God.*

Romans 5:10 — *Since our friendship with God was restored by the death of his Son while we were still his enemies, we will certainly be saved through the life of his Son.*

Roman 8:16 — *His Spirit joins with our spirit to affirm that we are God's children.*

1 John 3:2 — *Dear friends, we are already God's children, but he has not yet shown us what we will be like when Christ appears. But we do know that we will be like him, for we will see him as he really is.*

2 Corinthians 5:17 — *This means that anyone who belongs to Christ has become a new person. The old life is gone; a new life has begun!*

Ezekiel 11:19 — *I will give them singleness of heart and put a new spirit within them. I will take away their stony, stubborn heart and give them a tender, responsive heart.*

The Whole Armor of God

Ephesians 6:10-17 — *A final word: Be strong in the Lord and in his mighty power. Put on all of God's armor so that you will be able to stand firm against all strategies of the devil. For we are not fighting against flesh-and-blood enemies, but against evil rulers and authorities of the unseen world, against mighty powers in this dark world, and against evil spirits in the heavenly places. Therefore, put on every piece of God's armor so you will be able to resist the enemy in the time of evil. Then after the battle you will still be standing firm. Stand your ground, putting on the belt of truth and the body armor of God's righteousness. For shoes, put on the peace that comes from the Good News so that you will be fully prepared. In addition to all of these, hold up the shield of faith to stop the fiery arrows of the devil. Put on salvation as your helmet, and take the sword of the Spirit, which is the word of God.*

Psalm 103:10-14 — He does not punish us for all our sins; he does not deal harshly with us, as we deserve. For his unfailing love toward those who fear him is as great as the height of the heavens above the earth. He has removed our sins as far from us as the east is from the west. The Lord is like a father to his children, tender and compassionate to those who fear him. For he knows how weak we are; he remembers we are only dust.

Luke 7:48 — Then Jesus said to the woman, "Your sins are forgiven."

1 John 1:9 — If we confess our sins to him, he is faithful and just to forgive us our sins and to cleanse us from all wickedness.

Romans 8:1-2 — There is no condemnation for those who belong to Christ Jesus. And because you belong to him, the power of the life-giving Spirit has freed you from the power of sin that leads to death.

John 10:29 — I give them eternal life, and they will never perish. No one can snatch them away from me.

Romans 8:38-39 — I am convinced that nothing can ever separate us from God's love. Neither death nor life, neither angels nor demons, neither our fears for today nor our worries about tomorrow—not even the powers of hell can separate us from God's love. No power in the sky above or in the earth below—indeed, nothing in all creation will ever be able to separate us from the love of God that is revealed in Christ Jesus our Lord.

Hebrews 11:1 — Faith is the confidence that what we hope for will actually happen; it gives us assurance about things we cannot see.

Romans 8:25 — But if we look forward to something we don't yet have, we must wait patiently and confidently.

Titus 2:13 — While we look forward with hope to that wonderful day when the glory of our great God and Savior, Jesus Christ, will be revealed.

Ephesians 2:8 — God saved you by his grace when you believed. And you can't take credit for this; it is a gift from God.

Acts 1:8 — You will receive power when the Holy Spirit comes upon you. And you will be my witnesses, telling people about me everywhere—in Jerusalem, throughout Judea, in Samaria, and to the ends of the earth.

1 John 2:27 — *You have received the Holy Spirit, and he lives within you, so you don't need anyone to teach you what is true. For the Spirit teaches you everything you need to know, and what he teaches is true—it is not a lie. So just as he has taught you, remain in fellowship with Christ.*

John 14:26 — *But when the Father sends the Advocate as my representative—that is, the Holy Spirit—he will teach you everything and will remind you of everything I have told you.*

1 Corinthians 6:19 — *Don't you realize that your body is the temple of the Holy Spirit, who lives in you and was given to you by God? You do not belong to yourself.*

1 John 2:27 — *You have received the Holy Spirit, and he lives within you, so you don't need anyone to teach you what is true. For the Spirit teaches you everything you need to know, and what he teaches is true—it is not a lie. So just as he has taught you, remain in fellowship with Christ.*

Ephesians 1:13-14 — *Now you Gentiles have also heard the truth, the Good News that God saves you. And when you believed in Christ, he identified you as his own by giving you the Holy Spirit, whom he promised long ago. The Spirit is God's guarantee that he will give us the inheritance he promised and that he has purchased us to be his own people. He did this so we would praise and glorify him.*

Romans 12:6-8 — *In his grace, God has given us different gifts for doing certain things well. So if God has given you the ability to prophesy, speak out with as much faith as God has given you. If your gift is serving others, serve them well. If you are a teacher, teach well. If your gift is to encourage others, be encouraging. If it is giving, give generously. If God has given you leadership ability, take the responsibility seriously. And if you have a gift for showing kindness to others, do it gladly.*

1 Peter 4:10-11— *God has given each of you a gift from his great variety of spiritual gifts. Use them well to serve one another.* [11] *Do you have the gift of speaking? Then speak as though God himself were speaking through you. Do you have the gift of helping others? Do it with all the strength and energy that God supplies. Then everything you do will bring glory to God through Jesus Christ. All glory and power to him forever and ever! Amen.*

1 Corinthians 12:4-7 — *There are different kinds of spiritual gifts, but the same Spirit is the source of them all. There are different kinds of service, but we serve the same Lord. God works in different ways, but it is the same God who does the work in all of us. A spiritual gift is given to each of us so we can help each other.*

Hebrews 13:5 — *For God has said, I will never fail you. I will never abandon you.*

Joshua 1:5 — *For I will be with you as I was with Moses. I will not fail you or abandon you.*

Deuteronomy 31:6 — *For the Lord your God will personally go ahead of you. He will neither fail you nor abandon you.*

Psalm 27:10 — *Even if my father and mother abandon me, the Lord will hold me close.*

John 16:33 — *I have told you all this so that you may have peace in me. Here on earth you will have many trials and sorrows. But take heart, because I have overcome the world."*

2 Thessalonians 3:16 — *Now may the Lord of peace himself give you his peace at all times and in every situation. The Lord be with you all.*

Isaiah 26:3 — *You will keep in perfect peace all who trust in you, all whose thoughts are fixed on you!*

Colossians 3:15 — *And let the peace that comes from Christ rule in your hearts. For as members of one body you are called to live in peace. And always be thankful.*

Philippians 4:6-7 — *Don't worry about anything; instead, pray about everything. Tell God what you need, and thank him for all he has done. Then you will experience God's peace, which exceeds anything we can understand. His peace will guard your hearts and minds as you live in Christ Jesus.*

Psalm 37:4 — *Take delight in the Lord, and he will give you your heart's desires.*

Romans 6:23 — *The free gift of God is eternal life through Christ Jesus our Lord.*

1 Peter 2:9 — *You are not like that, for you are a chosen people. You are royal priests, a holy nation, God's very own possession. As a result, you can show others the goodness of God, for he called you out of the darkness into his wonderful light.*

2 Corinthians 5:20 — *We are Christ's ambassadors; God is making his appeal through us. We speak for Christ when we plead, "Come back to God!"*

Psalm 147:3 — *He heals the brokenhearted and binds up their wounds.*

James 5:15-16 — *Such a prayer offered in faith will heal the sick, and the Lord will make you well. And if you have committed any sins, you will be forgiven. Confess your sins to each other and pray for each other so that you may be healed. The earnest prayer of a righteous person has great power and produces wonderful results.*

Jeremiah 30:17 — *I will give you back your health and heal your wounds," says the Lord.*

1 Peter 2:24 — *He personally carried our sins in his body on the cross so that we can be dead to sin and live for what is right. By his wounds you are healed.*

Psalm 147:3 — *He heals the brokenhearted and binds up their wounds.*

John 3:16 — *For this is how God loved the world: He gave his one and only Son, so that everyone who believes in him will not perish but have eternal life.*

John 10:28 — *I give them eternal life, and they will never perish. No one can snatch them away from me.*

John 3:16 — *God loved the world so much that he gave his one and only Son, so that everyone who believes in him will not perish but have eternal life.*

John 10:29 — *My Father has given them to me, and he is more powerful than anyone else. No one can snatch them from the Father's hand.*

John 14:2 — *There is more than enough room in my Father's home. If this were not so, would I have told you that I am going to prepare a place for you?*

Revelation 21:4 — *He will wipe every tear from their eyes, and there will be no more death or sorrow or crying or pain. All these things are gone forever.*

Ephesians 2:10 — *We are God's masterpiece. He has created us anew in Christ Jesus, so we can do the good things he planned for us long ago.*

Psalm 150:4 — Praise him with the tambourine and dancing; praise him with strings and flutes!

John 10:10 — The thief's purpose is to steal and kill and destroy. My purpose is to give them a rich and satisfying life.

Chapter 22

The Salvation Prayer
Dear Lord Jesus, I believe you are truly the Son of God. I know that I am a sinner, and I ask for your forgiveness. I believe you died to pay the debt for my sins. I thank you for saving me. I trust you and I will follow you for all my days as my Savior. Help me to live a life pleasing to you. Amen.

Chapter 23

Ecclesiastes 3:1-8 — For everything there is a season, a time for every activity under heaven. A time to be born and a time to die. A time to plant and a time to harvest. A time to kill and a time to heal. A time to tear down and a time to build up. A time to cry and a time to laugh. A time to grieve and a time to dance. A time to scatter stones and a time to gather stones. A time to embrace and a time to turn away. A time to search and a time to quit searching. A time to keep and a time to throw away. A time to tear and a time to mend. A time to be quiet and a time to speak. A time to love and a time to hate. A time for war and a time for peace.

Luke 13:11-13 — He saw a woman who had been crippled by an evil spirit. She had been bent double for eighteen years and was unable to stand up straight. When Jesus saw her, he called her over and said, "Dear woman, you are healed of your sickness!" Then he touched her, and instantly she could stand straight. How she praised God!

Genesis 50:20 — You intended to harm me, but God intended it all for good. He brought me to this position so I could save the lives of many people.

Chapter 24

Psalm 23

The Lord is my shepherd; I have all that I need. He lets me rest in green meadows; he leads me beside peaceful streams. He renews my strength. He guides me along right paths, bringing honor to his name. Even when I walk through the darkest valley, I will not be afraid, for you are close beside me. Your rod and your staff protect and comfort me. You prepare a feast for me in the presence of my enemies. You honor me by anointing my head with oil. My cup overflows with blessings. Surely your goodness and unfailing love will pursue me all the days of my life, and I will live in the house of the Lord forever.

Chapter 25

John 8:44 — He was a murderer from the beginning. He has always hated the truth, because there is no truth in him. When he lies, it is consistent with his character; for he is a liar and the father of lies.

Author's Notes

I have included these notes for several reasons:

1. The information may help readers who have experienced similar events in their lives.
2. The information provides theories and symptoms regarding mental health difficulties. I hope it serves to show that every person in this book was not a "bad" person, but was suffering many forms of dysfunctional and harmful symptoms from their own experiences. When we understand, it is easier to forgive.
3. The information may help people understand why they or another person makes recurrent bad choices.
4. Scripture speaks to the miracle of my new life. The brain and heart can be healed and transformed.

Abortion: If you have been hurt by a past abortion and long to see yourself fully restored, visit StandForLife.org and watch the video from Someone Cares, a post-abortion restoration ministry.

Addictions: Addictions can develop when you continually attempt to sooth and comfort yourself rather than resolve the source of your pain. Many do not even know what is causing their pain. The root of addiction is the *need to be loved*. When you feel unloved and deprived, a longing and emptiness is triggered that you want to fill. A rush of dopamine from something like cocaine gives you a momentary burst of pleasure (dopamine), but when it wears off, you fall far down into the same feelings and problems you had when you took it. You can never satisfy an internal longing externally. There will never be enough of anything to do that. But you may go from one temporary fix to another, as I did.

Anna Sewell: I include Anna Sewell's story because her book *Black Beauty* had a profound influence on my life regarding the care and protection of animals. She was born in England (1820) into a devout Quaker family. She was largely educated at home by their mother due to a lack of money for schooling. At fourteen, she slipped and severely injured both ankles. For the rest of her life, she could not stand or walk for any length of time. For mobility, she used horse drawn carriages which contributed to her love of horses and concern for the humane treatment of animals.

Her mother expressed her religious faith most noticeably by authoring a series of evangelical children's books, which Sewell helped to edit. Anna wrote the manuscript to *Black Beauty* over a period of six years. During this time, she was so weak she could only write on slips of paper, which her mother then transcribed.

Her book is the first to be written from the perspective of an animal. Her aim was to "induce kindness, sympathy, and an understanding treatment of horses." Although the book is now considered a children's classic, it is considered to have had an effect on reducing cruelty to horses.

Battered Woman Syndrome: People who find themselves in an abusive relationship do not feel safe or happy, yet in many cases, they feel unable to leave. One prevalent reason is a belief that they are the cause of the abuse. Psychotherapist Lenore Walker developed the concept of battered woman syndrome (BWS) in the late 1970s. Walker noted that the patterns of behavior that result from abuse often resemble those of post-traumatic stress disorder and describes the battered woman syndrome as a subtype of PTSD. Most men and women who are abused physically or are humiliated orally report feeling worthless and embarrassed. They usually love the person who is harming them and believe they will change. It is difficult for someone outside the relationship to understand why the victim refuses to leave the relationship. When things are calm, the person being abused may still elevate and idealize the person who harms them, and believe things can get better. They often believe they deserve the abuse. The type of abuse I suffered with my husband mostly involved the psychological abuse of humiliation, blame, and criticism. Our physical shoving and struggling would be considered abusive by both of us. If you are in an abusive relationship, mental or physical, help is available. If you or someone you know is in immediate danger, calling 911 may help protect them from serious harm.

The National Domestic Violence Hotline offers online and phone help, as well as access to local resources. Call 800-799-7233 for immediate assistance. They also have a chat line at http://www.thehotline.org/what-is-live-chat/.

The National Dating Abuse Hotline number is 866-331-9474. Their chat line is http://www.loveisrespect.org//

Child Abuse: There are many types of abuse: physical, psychological, sexual, and spiritual. Overt abuse is pretty easy to determine—hitting, yelling, ridicule, name-calling, and other types of shaming. But neglect, for example, is one of the most abusive experiences a child can endure. Expecting perfection of a child is extremely abusive. There are other types of covert abuse that are important to identify. If you have any questions about covert abuse, a plethora of information can be found on the Internet. It is difficult to protect our children from things they shouldn't hear and see in this culture, but we must try and should be ready with explanations about things they need to understand.

Co-dependency: An over-simplified definition is that one has an excessive emotional or psychological reliance on another person. The object of their reliance has their primary interest elsewhere, on a substance, a process (making money, for example) or another person. The co-dependent person seeks after them ("the back walking away") for attention. The term was originally applied to the spouses of alcoholics, but the dynamics involved in these relationships have been found to be prevalent in the general population.

In general, the co-dependent partner in these relationships has lower self-esteem, poor boundaries, immature reactions, and are wonderful care-takers (to their own detriment).

Defense Mechanisms: An unconscious method to separate the mind from unwanted thoughts, painful memories, and irrational beliefs that would upset you. Instead of facing them, you may unconsciously choose to hide them in hope of forgetting about them most of the time, if not entirely. My mother used many defense mechanisms to help her cope with an unhappy life, and denial was one defense mechanism that protected her from "remembering" her past. Because she was never willing to recognize and face her demons and self-deception, she lived her life in darkness. I have often said, "My mother died with her song in her." At an early age, I unconsciously discovered how to create an alternate reality using defense mechanisms. It probably kept me from more severe psychiatric symptoms.

Depression: When you are depressed, your thinking is greatly impaired. Depression is not just linked to feelings of sadness, guilt, hopelessness, or even thoughts of suicide. It may affect a person physically as well as emotionally. Depression hurts all over. The symptoms may include fatigue, disturbance in sleep patterns, appetite, uneasiness in the abdomen, irregular bowel, difficulty concentrating, loss of motivation, and the most commonly reported symptoms feelings of sadness and irritability.

Emotional Incest: A dynamic that occurs in parenting where the parent seeks emotional support through the child, when it should be sought through an adult relationship. The child's developmental needs are ignored. The effects of emotional incest can be similar to those resulting from physical incest. This phenomenon is also "spousification," which refers to a dynamic in which parents turn to children for emotional support while ignoring the child's developmental needs. When parents replace their partner with his or her own child in order to meet emotional needs, the relationship becomes exploitative in which the parents' expectations exceed the child's ability to meet them.

Nightmare Disorder: A nightmare is a disturbing dream associated with negative feelings, such as anxiety or fear that awakens you. Although nightmares are common, nightmare disorder happens when nightmares are frequent, maybe repetitive. They are extremely vivid, cause upset and distress, disrupt sleep, and use problems with daytime functioning or create fear of going to sleep. The nightmare's storyline is usually related to threats to safety or survival. When you awaken, you feel scared, anxious, angry, sad, or disgusted as a result of your dream. These feelings may persist during the day. It is not easy to fall back to sleep, and as a result, the person experiences daytime sleepiness and lack of concentration. This is a common occurrence in both adult and childhood post-traumatic stress disorder. For some people, reading scary books or watching frightening movies, especially before bed, can be associated with nightmares. Unfortunately, without proper guidance, the Bible was a scary book to me as a child.

Nurturing: Perhaps the single most-important ability that helps one live in harmony and happiness. A gentle touch is most often thought of when nurturing is discussed. Early and continual parent-child touch has been studied for generations. Children who experience warm and gentle touch develop and maintain healthy relationships throughout their lives through a strong and healthy sense of self. When one has been raised with feelings of attachment in a family, then one has felt unconditionally loved. Trust and respect are necessary to feeling loved too.

Knowing what to expect of children as they reach physical, emotional, and intellectual milestones is important in the development of children's positive self-worth. When parents make demands that children are unable to meet, or they make no demands and have no expectations, then the children's overall feelings of worth are lowered. People must learn to have a gentle touch with all things.

In addition to nurturing, there are other characteristics of good parenting:

- Children deserve to be celebrated. What children observe from your behavior is more important than anything you will ever say.

- Quality time and attention are the most important gifts you will ever give your children.

- Do not burden your children with your problems. Handle grown-up problems with other grown-ups.

- Encourage your child's unique gifts. Empower them to reach their dreams.

- A child's body and thoughts are to be respected at all times. Disrespect of any kind is *never* okay.

- You are only human, and as such, you will make mistakes. Apologize to your children, and be intentional about not making the same mistake again. Children want to forgive.

- One of the most important gifts you can give your children is to take care of yourself.

- Age appropriate rules are important to a sense of security. Follow through with natural and consistent consequences so that children know what to expect.

- Be a model of gratitude.
- Regardless of the age of the child, express your love for them frequently.
- Teach the importance of rest and balance. Our society is too stressful.
- Be silly.

Postpartum Depression (PPD), also called "Baby Blues," is a type of mood disorder associated with childbirth. Onset can be immediate. Symptoms include extreme sadness, low energy, anxiety, crying, and irritability toward the child and others. This illness must be taken seriously and help provided. Roughly 15 percent of these women are affected by postpartum psychosis—one of the leading causes of the murder of children less than one year old.

Post-traumatic stress disorder (PTSD)—childhood induced: It is well documented that children who were abused suffer from their own form of PTSD symptoms. These children often use drugs and alcohol to cope with their distress. A range of persistent psychiatric disorders may also occur—panic attacks, phobias, intense unstable relationships, feelings of emptiness, and identity confusion. General impulsivity, self-destructive behavior, delinquency, anxiety, depression, and suicidal thoughts are common issues suffered by victims of abuse. These problems can show themselves in childhood and early adolescence.

Post-traumatic stress disorder PTSD—Military: Anger and irritability are hyper-arousal symptoms of PTSD. It has become clear that veterans are at risk for a number of mental health problems, including PTSD and extreme anger. Research has found a connection between PTSD and relationship violence. Although my father never turned his physical anger on my mother or myself, anyone or anything else was in danger during his episodes. In the most severe cases of military or other PTSD causes, a dissociative identity disorder often described as "Dr. Jekyll and Mr. Hyde" can occur.

Re-parenting: Many current articles are available on re-parenting, also called "healing the mother wound." This type of therapy refers to your psychotherapist taking the role of a concerned and trustworthy parent so you can learn what a trusting relationship is like. It is based on the belief that many psychological issues stem from a child growing up without his or her needs being met.

Shame: Just as the source of shame can be all forms of abuse or neglect, shame is not just one feeling but many. It is a cluster of feelings and experiences. These can include:

- Feeling humiliated.
- Feeling impotent. When a child realizes there is nothing he can do to stop the abuse, he feels powerless, helpless. This can also lead to his always feeling unsafe, even long after the abuse has stopped.
- Feelings defective. Most victims of abuse report feeling defective, damaged, or corrupted following the experience of being abused.
- Feelings alienated and isolated: feeling different, less-than, damaged, or cast out. And while victims may long to talk to someone about their inner pain, they often feel immobilized, trapped, and alone in their shame.
- Self-blame. Victims almost always blame themselves for being abused and being shamed. This is particularly true when abuse happens or begins in childhood.

- Feeling rage. Rage almost always follows being shamed. It serves a much-needed self-protective function of both insulating the self against further exposure and actively keeping others away.
- Fear, hurt, distress, or rage can also accompany or follow shame experiences as secondary reactions. For example, feeling exposed is often followed by the fear of further exposure and further occurrences of shame. Rage protects the self against further exposure.

References on Shame:

- Pia Mellody: *Co-dependent No More*
- Pia Mellody: *5 Core Symptoms*
- John Bradshaw: *Healing the Shame that Binds*
- Brené Brown: Women and Shame

If you suspect you are a victim of Debilitating Shame due to Childhood Abuse, you may want to take the following questionnaire:

1. *Do you blame yourself for the abuse you experienced as a child?*

2. *Do you believe your parent (or other adult or older child) wouldn't have abused you if you hadn't pushed him or her into doing it?*

3. *Do you believe you were a difficult, stubborn, or selfish child who deserved the abuse you received?*

4. *Do you believe you made it difficult for your parents or others to love you?*

5. *Do you believe you were a disappointment to your parents or family?*

6. *Do you feel you are basically unlovable?*

7. *Do you have a powerful inner critic who finds fault with nearly everything you do?*

8. *Are you a perfectionist?*

9. *Do you believe you don't deserve to be happy, loved, or successful?*

10. *Do you have a difficult time believing someone could love you?*

11. *Do you push away people who are good to you?*

12. *Are you afraid that if people really get to know you, they won't like or accept you? Do you feel like a fraud?*

13. *Do you believe that anyone who likes or loves you has something wrong with them?*

14. *Do you feel like a failure in life?*

15. *Do you hate yourself?*

16. *Do you feel ugly—inside and out?*

17. *Do you hate your body?*

18. *Do you believe the only way someone can like you is if you do everything they want?*

19. *Are you a people pleaser?*

20. *Do you censor yourself when you talk to other people, always being careful not to offend them or hurt their feelings?*

21. *Do you feel like the only thing you have to offer is your sexuality?*

22. *Are you addicted to alcohol, drugs, sex, pornography, shopping, gambling, or stealing, or do you suffer from any other addiction?*

23. *Do you find it nearly impossible to admit when you are wrong or when you've made a mistake?*

24. *Do you feel bad about the way you've treated people?*

25. *Are you afraid of what you're capable of doing?*

26. *Are you afraid of your tendency to be abusive—either verbally, emotionally, physically, or sexually?*

27. *Have you been in one or more relationships where you were abused either verbally, emotionally, physically, or sexually?*

28. *Did you or do you feel you deserved the abuse?*

29. *Do you always blame yourself if something goes wrong in a relationship?*

30. *Do you feel like it isn't worth trying because you'll only fail?*

31. *Do you sabotage your happiness, your relationships, or your success?*

32. *Are you self-destructive (engaging in acts of self-harm, driving recklessly, suicidal attempts, and so on)?*

33. *Do you feel inferior to or less than other people?*

34. *Do you often lie about your accomplishments or your history in order to make yourself look better in others' eyes?*

35. *Do you neglect your body, your health, or your emotional needs (not eating right, not getting enough sleep, not taking care of your medical or dental needs)?*

There isn't any formal scoring for this questionnaire, but if you answered yes to many of these questions, you can be assured that you are suffering some debilitating shame. Your answers can also help you identify areas of your life that may need attention.

Additional resources for learning more about any of these topics can be found at PsychologyToday.com and PsychCentral.com.

About the Author

Dr. Anne Worth is a Christian counselor, author, and speaker. She is a member of the Highland Country Fellowship Church in Dallas, Texas. For several years, she has been of service to the homeless population and Sudanese refugees in her community. Dr. Anne also has a heart for animals and enjoys fostering dogs until they find a good home. As a hobby, she creates crosses and other Christian art using vintage jewelry.

DrAnneWorthAuthor.com
AnneWorthDr@att.net

Made in the USA
Coppell, TX
02 August 2022